THE OFFICIAL STOCKBROKER'S HANDBOOK

THE
OFFICIAL
STOCKBROKER'S
HANDBOOK

Peter Cohn
and
Douglas Miller

A PERIGEE BOOK

Perigee Books
are published by
The Putnam Publishing Group
200 Madison Avenue
New York, NY 10016

Design: Susan Brooker/Levavi & Levavi
Cartoons: James Sherman

Library of Congress Cataloging-in-Publication Data

Cohn, Peter.
    The official stockbroker's handbook.

    "A Perigee book."
    1. Stock-exchange—Anecdotes, facetiae, satire, etc.
I. Miller, Douglas, date.   II. Title.
PN6231.S73C64   1986   818'.5402   86-4870
ISBN 0-399-51180-6

Printed in the United States of America

1   2   3   4   5   6   7   8   9   10

This is a work of fiction. The events described are imaginary and the characters are fictitious and not intended to represent specific living persons. When persons are referred to by their true names, they are portrayed in entirely fictitious settings and incidents; it is not intended that any reader infer that these settings and incidents are real or that the events ever actually happened.

In addition to Stephen R. Brown, our photographer, we would like to thank the following individuals and organizations for providing props or pictures.

The American Film Institute

C & P Telephone Co.

The Chicago Mercantile Exchange

King World Productions

The Library of Congress
(The George G. Bain Collection)

The Maryland Corporation for Public Broadcasting

NASA

The National Archives

The National Cattleman's Association

The National Museum of American History

Quotron Inc.

Susan Krenn (our model-rocket builder)

The United States Treasury Department

Voss & Co.

Western Union Inc.

All Curb Market photos are from the George G. Bain Collection of the Library of Congress.

The MX Dart is a Stephen R. Brown photo.

CONTENTS

INTRODUCTION

Have you ever met a little kid who wanted to grow up to be a stockbroker?

Probably not. But any tot who greedily looks at a playmate's flashier toys has made the first step toward a career in financial services. Soon simple envy for Jimmy's red fire truck or Jenny's dollhouse turns into an uncontrollable lust for wealth. Many of these precocious, acquisitive personalities eventually fail to marry well, get into law school or master the art of dunking a basketball.

It is then that they realize Wall Street is their destiny, and must ask: "Where the heck is Wall Street, anyway?"

For generations it was located on the southern tip of Manhattan. But now "the Street" is more than just a place—it is the vast array of firms engaged in buying, selling or creating financial products across the nation.

Stockbrokers are the people who are the licensed registered representatives (RRs) of these firms.

For centuries stockbrokers were also known as

Do you know where Wall Street is?

customer's men. This meant that they were, in fact, men who, in exchange for investment advice, earned commissions on the securities transactions of their customers.

Today's brokers tend to bridle at the term "customer's man." This is because many of them are women, and because all of them dislike the servile implications of the term. Some brokers like to call themselves "account executives." Others go for the title of "financial consultant." A few are happy simply to be known as "securities salesmen."

Whatever you want to call them, brokers remain a mystery to most people. Except in rare instances of theft, fraud or embezzlement, retail stockbrokers seldom make the news—let alone history.

And when history does bring the brokerage business into its sweep, it's always because of a recession, depression or market crash. It is then that brokers are labeled "parasites" and are called to testify before Congress.

Fame is not what an RR wants. A stockbroker wants money. In 1985 the average retail producer netted $80,000—not bad for a bunch of nobodies. And with *The Official Stockbroker's Handbook* and a little practice, anybody can become a nobody earning big bucks on Wall Street.

CHAPTER·1

DO YOU REALLY WANT TO MAKE A LOT OF MONEY?

Until just a few years ago, stockbroking was an exclusive rich man's club. Old-line regional investment firms controlled the business. Brokers came from the ranks of the Establishment. And in all too many cases, the wealthy used the brokerage industry as the dumping ground for their wayward sons (and these same sons as the dumping ground for their wayward daughters).

Success came easy. Brokers would simply rely on old-school ties, social connections and family referrals. "Are you white?" and "Are you nice?" were the only two questions on a broker's job application test.

Then came the 1970s, the decade of the Financial Services Revolution. The backdrop was economic turmoil, as the roller coaster of inflation and recession made obsolete the traditionally passive and conservative approach to investing. In 1975 the New York Stock Exchange abolished its long-standing system of "fixed-rate" commissions, ushering in a new era of competition among stockbrokers. As overall financial deregulation proceeded, banks, insurance companies and other new competitors rushed into the once-protected securities industry.

Brokerage firms had to slash costs, spend millions on new computer systems and hire aggressive salespeople to compete. The result: an industry dominated by diversified financial services companies that sell financial products the way McDonald's sells hamburgers.

Today brokerage firms want business from anyone with money. And they need salespeople to make contact, to find that common ground between seller and consumer—better known as retail markup. In other words, they need *you*.

Whether you're fresh out of college or forty-five, desperate and ready to make a change, you can find your fortune in the nation's fast-est-growing business: financial services.

Here are a few real-life stories from people who have already made the move:

☐ "When I was a loyal corporate manager, my only inflation hedge was a roll of eighteen-cent stamps. Now that I'm in investments full-time, *I* am my most valuable financial asset."

☐ "I had a 4.0 grade point average in college, but ended up as nothing more than a glorified secretary. Now my sales assistant Bruce makes the coffee every morning."

☐ "Financial services sounded great, but I never thought it was for me. Was I wrong! I've already lost thirty pounds and my liver spots have disappeared!"

☐ "I was working sixty hours a week as an associate at a corporate law firm, with no partnership

in sight. Now I make twice the money for half the work. I *read* boilerplate instead of write it."

Perhaps you're wondering if you have what it takes to make it in financial services. You can find out by asking yourself one simple question: "Do I want to make a lot of money?" If the answer is "yes" or even "maybe," you're in luck. Besides the simple desire to get rich, the only other things you'll need to get started are a suit, a blow dryer and a stack of fresh business cards.

Other than huge, six-figure incomes, what are

some of the other benefits enjoyed by most brokers? Here are just a few:

☐ A fully equipped, well-lit and asbestos-free office.
☐ A personal, toll-free "800" phone number.
☐ Enough conversational fodder to make you a star at the cocktail party or disco of your choice.
☐ An impressive-sounding title, usually vice president, that tells the world that you're an achiever.

Not too bad when you consider that all you have to do is show up at the office occasionally, talk on the phone and watch a TV set all day. "Don't work hard, work smart" will be your motto.

But how do you get started? What's the best way to land your first job? How do you get a license to sell securities? How do you survive until the commissions start rolling in? And who's going to empty your trash and post your bail?

Sell Yourself into a Job

In the brokerage game, "résumé" is just a fancy French word that means "get off your duff and get moving."

Earnest cover letters, fake transcripts and recommendations from your high school athletic coach won't get you a job selling securities.

To get hired by a brokerage firm, you have to prove that you're a hard-charging salesman. And the first thing you have to sell is you!

Your potential customer is the branch office manager of the securities firm you want to join. He's the one who does the hiring. Branch managers were once salesmen themselves (before they kicked themselves upstairs to cushy management positions), so it's only natural that what they're looking for is salesmanship.

Hungry mouths to feed at home make for a hungry, motivated broker at the office.

"If some kid walks in off the street and starts chewing my ear off about how he wants a job because he's interested in the economy and financial markets, it's a definite turnoff," comments one Florida branch manager. "I remember one sucker who came in and showed me his stock-charting system. I turned him over to a junior broker as a potential client. That job interview ended up costing the poor fella his $200,000 inheritance."

Managers want motivated people who can sell with impunity. They respond particularly well to total desperation. If you have seven kids, a big house, and are up to your neck in debt, by all means be candid—a manager will see you as someone unlikely to suffer from motivational difficulty when it comes time to pick up a phone and sell.

Even if you're single and debt-free, a confident smile and an honest belief in your-self will do the trick. If the first manager you meet laughs in your face, take down his license plate number and get even later. Remember, your goal isn't to get a job. Your goal is to make money. . . Now!

What Firm to Work for and When's the Best Time to Look

Sadly, many otherwise intelligent people think brokerage companies hire only during bull markets.

Although it's true that brokers make more money when the market is hot and trading volume high, you can get a job even if the Dow has dropped below 700. During bear markets, an office manager needs all the brokers he can get to generate enough revenue to pay the office overhead (and his inflated salary).

A true self-starter can seize an opportunity in any market environment. No matter when you start looking, in an office employing forty brokers—a typical

"*Too bad we don't work for Merrill Lynch!*"

number for a branch—you can usually see an empty desk or two. A closer examination of the furnishings may reveal shell-shocked brokers hiding under the desks, but generally you can assume the manager is still looking for new salesmen.

Younger job seekers without employment experience stand the best chance at smaller, regional firms. Many of the major national firms look at the regional firms as farm teams, hiring brokers away once they learn the basics and begin to produce.

However, don't shy away from the big firms. Most of them have organized recruitment and training programs that are often open to youthful applicants.

Don't waste your time seeking out a job at one of the prestigious, so-called "white-shoe" firms primarily involved in investment banking activities and dealings with major financial institutions. You want to start in the trenches of retail selling.

So get your hands dirty by digging for employment opportunities. Begin each morning by doing what real stockbrokers do—read the newspaper, scouring every scrap of news and advertising copy for likely prospects.

Start with the business section. Answering any ad for municipal bonds, tax shelters or growth-stock portfolios could actually make you rich. Why? Because every investment come-on is a job lead for you.

R.S.V.P. any invitation to an investment seminar. These peculiar exercises in investment marketing will never bore you since you will be doing the buttonholing. Load up on hors d'oeuvres and casually press the flesh with potential

"A clean, well-lit asbestos-free office."

bosses and colleagues (see chapter 2 for more details).

Read between the lines when you're looking at the help-wanteds. Brokerage companies never want to let the general public know they need help. This could set off a financial panic. Thus all brokerage industry employment ads are in code. "I applied for a job as a short-order cook, but ended up selling utility bonds," recalls one pleasantly surprised Florida teenager.

Also look in the "for sale" section under "garage sales." Any ad offering typewriters, copying machines, news tickers and other office equipment is probably a smart office manager trying to make some extra money. If you can find this out, you're guaranteed a job—and a corner office.

The newspaper's only one of the many places you can turn to for valuable job-finding leads. Be creative! Get a job selling BMWs so you can meet brokers. Run for vice president and lose. Sit on a flagpole and tell the media that you won't come down until you can join Merrill Lynch.

Before you know it, your persistence will pay off. Some manager will offer you a job and then suddenly you'll have to ask yourself, "Should I take it?" The answer is yes, because once you have a job selling securities, you can always get a better one.

Full Disclosure

All new brokers must submit to one extremely sobering bureaucratic detail— completing the Uniform Application for Securities Registration (better known as the U-4 form).

The securities industry is the only private business that has anything like the U-4. It is a five-page application crammed with exacting questions about your whereabouts and activities over the past decade. You will need a magnifying glass to read the questions and a lawyer to tell you how to answer them.

This disclosure form sounds like it's the work of some intrusive government agency, but it's not. It's your future peers in the industry who came up with the U-4. Filling in the form will be your first contact with the National Association of Securities Dealers (NASD), the grim reaper of securities industry self-regulation.

The main point of this exercise is to let new brokers know that no chance for unlimited wealth exists without a corresponding possibility of long-term incarceration. The powers that be don't let other people get close to big money without checking them out first.

Even if you feel comfortable deceiving the government when you file taxes, apply for student loans or sign up for unemployment compensation, you'd better think twice about skirting the truth in the U-4. Any suspicious-looking answers will lead to a thorough investigation of your life by an army of private detectives.

As you read the questions, there will be no doubt in your mind that you have made a wise career decision. You'll know you must be getting near the mother lode of capitalism.

Two specific tips:

☐ Don't under any circumstances use your mechanical autograph machine to sign this form.

☐ Don't hide any of your previous aliases. This includes cute nicknames given to you by partners encountered during your swinging single days.

By the time you're done filling out this form, you can see why hyped-up résumés are a bad idea when you're trying to get a job as a broker.

One Broker's Carrot Is Another Rep's Stick

On day one of the new job, a shocking realization hits a starting broker: "Brokers get paid by commission, commissions are earned by selling securities, and up until yesterday I thought securities had something to do with burglar alarms."

Relax. Brokerage firms don't expect new producers to come charging out of the starting gate at full speed. But they do want you to move your legs.

Your established colleagues draw no salary and depend exclusively on commissions they make from selling investments. The broker's commission is known as a "net commission" or "payout," and represents a percentage of the firm's take on each sale, the "gross commission." Both gross and net commission rates vary from product to product. (See chapter 3 if you're so greedy you can't wait to find out how much you'll make.)

Any respectable firm offers an initial compensation package that pays a base salary until a new rep has a fair shot at making a living from commissions. Needless to say, these deals include plenty of incentives to prevent a come-in-late, leave-early attitude.

An industry-wide survey conducted by the Securities Industry Association found that in 1984 trainees typically started with a salary of somewhere between $1000 and $2000 a month (an $18,800 median annualized salary). Big firms paid their trainees significantly more.

YOUR WAY INTO A JOB, THE EASY WAY

When you're out job hunting, you can score big points with a potential boss by showing that you're confident and aggressive. One sure-fire approach is to walk into the office without an appointment. If you can get by his secretary, you can be sure that the manager will be impressed. Here are a few one-liners that always work:

☐ *Buenos días*, I would like to know if you accept large cash deposits and if you have a branch in Bogotá.

☐ Does anyone here own a Porsche? There's been a terrible accident.

☐ I've got some nylons and a Hershey bar, *Fräulein*.

☐ Help me, I'm networking.

☐ Good morning, Ms. Smith, I'm from the National Organization for Women and we're filing a sex-discrimination suit against your employer. I'd like to speak to your boss right away.

New brokers at firms in the $100-million-and-over category (as measured by total gross commissions) received an annualized median salary of $19,500. (Our own unofficial investigation also found that smaller firms require new brokers to pay for their own nondairy creamer, office supplies and telephone mouthpiece disinfectant—so be sure to plan your budget carefully).

You can expect to continue to draw a modest salary even after you are "registered," although your salary will probably phase out as your production mounts. At the same time, you'll probably see a carrot dangling in front of your face in the form of an increasing payout.

Can you bargain for more than just a company's basic trainee package? Yes, but only if you're moving into the brokerage business with some impressive credentials. A former IBM regional manager who left behind a $150,000 salary can bet his sweet bank account a manager will lay out the sausage.

Don't let the obvious risks of becoming a commission-driven entrepreneur get you down. Wage slavery is for the birds: unlimited income potential is the ticket in financial sales.

Training

Stockbroker boot camp doesn't mean a trip to Parris Island. Your most valuable training will take place right in your new office, as you struggle to familiarize yourself with the mechanics of the brokerage business (as described in your branch operations manual), read the other training literature provided by your firm, and begin to study for your Securities Industry Licensing Test, the "Series 7."

However, if you're a hot prospect with a new job at one of the big national brokerage companies, you may find yourself in an organized training program. Do yourself a favor and sign up for the optional classes in power lunching, dressing for success and the drafting of chain letters.

Enjoy your training because it's the only time your firm will play the role of kindly benefactor. The typical firm spent $12,000 per trainee on training expenses in 1984 (including salary, testing, registration fees, purchased training-course materials, housing, travel and employee benefits), according to the SIA report. The firms estimated that "indirect costs" like office supplies and phone bills came to another $4000 for each new broker. It's a perfect opportunity to catch up with your old elementary school pen pals in distant lands!

Again, big firms spend substantially more on training. Companies in the $100-million-plus category doled out $22,670, as opposed to the $17,300 laid out by the under–$10 million outfits.

The Series 7

Just as the legal profession has its bar exam, the brokerage profession requires new brokers to pass something called the "Series 7" before they can call themselves "registered reps."

The bar exam was designed by greedy lawyers seeking to limit the number of attorneys in practice.

Surprisingly enough, the brokerage business doesn't use its test to create a much-feared broker shortage. Instead, the Series 7 is simply a way for the industry to make sure that even the most abject morons entering the business know a little bit about economics, finance and keeping out of jail.

Compared to the bar exam, the Series 7 is like fishing for anchovies with dynamite.

A challenging battery of IQ tests keeps all but the brightest applicants out of the vital stock brokerage profession.

You must take the test ninety days after you're hired. Most firms only give you two chances to pass the 250-question multiple-choice exam.

The bigger brokerage houses provide their trainees with every possible test question—in advance. At a national firm, you will also be enlisted in a weekend cram course that has a 92 percent success rate.

If you work for a firm that doesn't have access to these handy resources, you're just going to have to do a little cramming. You can choose from a wide variety of coaching and self-preparation programs, including the popular new Series 7 videocassette featuring Jane Fonda.

You'll be glad to know that the Series 7 is run by the NASD (thank God for industry self-regulation!). The NASD administers dozens of securities industry exams taken by an estimated 500,000 people a year. Most of the NASD tests these days are taken on a computer at a user-friendly Control Data business office (although not at this time the Series 7). You don't have to be computer-literate to figure out how to take the tests, but electronic testing means that you won't find any crib notes in the trash can. However, if you wear 3-D glasses, you can make out the fingerprint impressions of the previous testee on the screen.

Speed-reading tip:
A large nose can cut your
daily reading time in half!

First-Year Indignities: After Eighteen Months of Hell, You'll Be Rich for the Rest of Your Life

Young doctors must suffer through grueling twenty-four-hour shifts in the emergency room. A junior lawyer must grind away for years before fighting corporate sharks in court. And, yes, starting stockbrokers also pay a steep price for their ascent into the upper reaches of our society.

Take for example the frequent mandatory "smiling and dialing" evening telemarketing marathons imposed on junior brokers by hard-driving managers. Imagine a dozen restless

young RRs put together in the office for a two-hour session of marathon unsolicited telephone sales calls. Add to that the obligatory pizza and beer keg, and you end up with an ugly food fight. Never wear your best suit to one of these glorified fraternity parties.

On a more sober note, it's usually very difficult for a new rep to get used to working in an open-space bullpen—the layout of almost all branch offices. You have to learn how to concentrate in a noisy, exposed environment in close quarters with fellow brokers. Never eavesdrop. If a veteran salesman catches you listening, NASD regulations require you to open an account with him.

Other potential problems arise from the sophisticated office technology you'll have to master. It may take you six months to find the on-off switch on your Quotron or to make sense out of the twenty-five flashing buttons on your phone console.

Then there's the inevita-ble office politics. You start out at the bottom of the totem pole, and everybody lets you know it. Some newly minted reps have been known to refer to their secretaries as "boss" in order to gain access to their own monthly client statements and commission runs.

A few other simple "dos" and "don'ts" will help you avoid some of the other pitfalls of your start-up phase:

☐ Always be at your desk before your manager walks in the door and always remain in the office until his taillights disappear from sight. If you're lucky, this will mean a 10 A.M. to 4:14 P.M. workday.

☐ Obtain your own business cards. If you wait for the company to do it, your name will be misspelled.

☐ Subscribe to major business publications and then immediately cancel. You will still receive sample replacement copies for ninety days.

☐Even if you are offered inside information straight from company analysts, never perform sexual favors for a junior sales assistant or other low-level employees (unless you're sure the information is reliable).

☐Destroy all your credit cards. Cash, better known as "fist money," is the currency of financial services reps. There's nothing like a huge wad of bills to project the image of a hell-for-leather stockbroker.

Shockbroker

All prospective brokers must put up with the Series 7. An unlucky but thankfully tiny minority of each new batch of customer's men faces something far more treacherous. It's called the Simulated Office Environment Test.

As part of a secret agreement with federal regulatory authorities, one out of every 5000 new brokers must submit to this grueling ordeal.

Designed by the same behavioral scientists who created shopping malls in the 1950s and rock music videos in the '80s, the test assaults the subject's senses to the outer limits of human tolerance. Only those who can continue to sell effectively during the onslaught survive.

The test begins at 5:30 A.M. You have a hangover. You are asked to enter the small test capsule, better known as the Skinner Cubicle.

As you attempt to make yourself comfortable in the hard-plastic pilot's seat, you must quickly familiarize yourself with the communications and data-processing equipment that leers at you in a user-unfriendly way.

Within thirty seconds, a voice starts barking instructions at you from squawk boxes placed around the cube. The first order: make a hundred outgoing phone calls in ten minutes. As you dial, you must continue to respond to orders that blare from the squawk boxes and flash on your Quotron. These orders will call for you to execute complicated trading maneuvers by tele-typing orders to fictitious brokers, traders, institutions and slush funds set up as part of the test. If you put any of these instructions on paper, you will immediately be ejected from the cube.

An exclusive photo shows an aspiring broker facing the challenge of the Simulated Office Environment Test.

You must know the meaning of "dumbbell swap," "butterfly hedge," and "net present value." You'll have to shoot from the hip and call forth your utmost reserves of personality and improvisatory risk-taking. These are your only weapons, because you've got to sell yourself out of the Skinner Cubicle.

To make matters worse, the cube is a vortex of inconveniences and discomfort. There are no secretaries to answer your phone. Pounding, piercing, deafening aural blasts come close to making you deafer than a heavy-metal drummer. You have no control over the cube temperature. Arctic air masses roar out of the air-conditioning ducts, only to be replaced by a raging heat comparable to a nuclear reactor in overdrive.

Sound familiar? It should: this is the closest approximation of an actual office environment science has ever devised.

As the test enters its second phase, you'll have to speed-read an eight-inch stack of worthless research reports and sales-program memos, and then cull through a forty-foot stream of computer printouts to find the error in your month-to-date commissions earned. At the same time you'll have to handle an endless series of "broker of the day" calls from little old ladies who are still confused by the AT&T split-up.

Suddenly the lights will go out and your senses will be assaulted by a blinding psychedelic light show. Your "cube" has been hit.

A grave voice comes over the speaker system. "Your firm, a simple broker dealer, has been acquired by a large, synergistic financial services conglomerate with long-run corporate plans for just one sales force. Unless you submit, you will be destroyed immediately with neutron weapons."

At this point all successful test subjects simply give up.

DANGEROUS EARLY WARNING SIGNALS

The eight early warning indicators that tell you a branch office is not for you:
- ☐ If the office manager is removing the Leroy Neiman prints from the wall when you walk in.
- ☐ If the receptionist is a burly, six-foot-tall Sicilian with a sawed-off shotgun.
- ☐ If even only one of the male brokers is wearing a ponytail and beads.
- ☐ If the firm has photos of recent investment banking successes such as the Erie Canal, the Hoover Dam and the Grand Canyon.
- ☐ If everybody in the room is taller, tanner and more Teutonic than you are.
- ☐ If local financial services executives are required to sit in the back of the bus or to use separate rest rooms.
- ☐ If any of the brokers are wearing scuffed shoes, a sure sign of dangerous laxity.

Giving the Finger: Prints Among Men

A final inconvenience in your preparation to join the ranks of the brokerage fraternity is a fingerprinting session at the local FBI office. All registered reps must keep their prints on file with the authorities, a provision that has virtually wiped out the possibility of embezzlement, wire fraud and other forms of financial shoplifting.

Because each state in which you plan to sell securities requires its own set of your prints, your session with the cops could go on all day. Don't get too relaxed: these tough guys will arrest

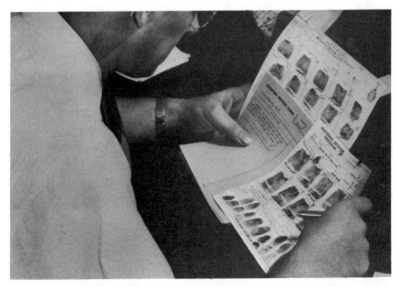

A vigilant G-man scrutinizes the fingerprints of a broker applicant.

you if you whistle "Puff the Magic Dragon" while being fingerprinted.

If you're smart, you can turn this ordeal into a valuable self-awareness exercise. Fingerprints can be more revealing than even your astrological sign or biorhythm chart. You'll surely find that those neat-looking patterns are far more than just a history of where your hands have been. The following are some sample fingerprint patterns, with explanations of what they may reveal about you.

This pattern results from too many afternoons spent on the golf course:

Yes, your print is a miniature replica of the fourteenth hole at the famed Augusta National Golf

Club. Keep playing, your sales pitch and putt are going to take you to the top of the industry.

Does the following remind you of the famed pork belly?

Sorry, but you're not destined to make a fortune in commodities. This is what the sidewalk will look like after you jump from your twenty-fifth-floor corner office.

You may want to call this an "upside breakout," but unfortunately this pattern reveals to the authorities that you are an escaped convict suffering from amnesia:

One final tip. It's well worth the money to have your nails professionally tended by a licensed manicurist before you're printed —applicants with cuticle deformities are automatically reported to higher authorities.

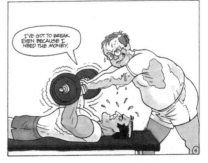

Dirty Tricks:
An Office Survival Guide

Office rivalries are natural in the competitive retail brokerage environment. If you don't decide to nail your enemy, your enemy will decide to nail you.

Try some of these dirty tricks to sabotage your rival. Keep at it and you'll inherit his best accounts. And if you're really ruthless, top executives at your firm will put you on the coveted management fast track.

So why wait?

Phase 1: Softening the Mark

☐ Fill his trash can with junk mail, old newspapers and cartons of day-old Chinese takeout.

☐ Eat a sticky bun and then fondle his telephone receiver.

☐ Remove his extra chair from the vicinity of his desk or office.

Phase 2: Escalation

☐ Answer all junk mail inquiries with his name and address. The volume of mail he receives will cripple his ability to use the incoming mail.

☐ Pay his sales assistant to help you address mailers. Not only will you benefit from the extra help, but your rival won't get any phone messages without paying for them.

☐ Before he runs his mass mailing through the office postage meter, reduce the postage value by a few cents.

Phase 3: Brutal Slugfest

☐ Send all his Jewish clients Christmas cards and all of his Christian clients Hanukkah cards.

☐ Put an unlicensed handgun in his briefcase right before he leaves for the airport on the way to an important out-of-town meeting.

☐ Get his wife/her husband drunk at the Christmas party and have her/him sit on the copying machine nude.

The Squawk Box

Unlike most denizens of the modern office, brokers don't spend the day listening to piped-in elevator music. Instead, customer's men are bombarded by nonstop information blasting through an office squawk box, a two-way cable radio providing continuous communications between the home office and the branch offices.

Up-to-the-minute news reports are the most popular programming on the box. Wars, assassinations, earthquakes, airplane crashes and epidemics are particularly well covered on most systems. Interviews with floor traders and analysts provide the color commentary.

But your firm doesn't maintain its communications system simply to keep its brokers entertained. Your firm needs the squawk boxes to move product. Thus there are frequent announcements of "specials," products your company is eager to get rid of.

Because most of this product information is already available to the branches from other sources—including a broker's Quotron and the in-house wire—it takes a

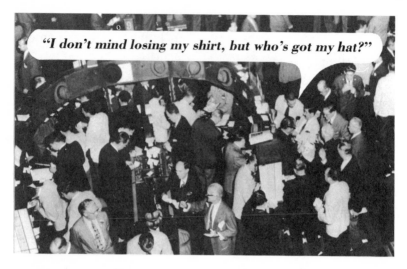

"*I don't mind losing my shirt, but who's got my hat?*"

little show-business pizzazz to keep brokers interested in product announcements.

When the head office really gets desperate to unload a product, the squawk box announces sales contests, with golf umbrellas, tote bags, company ties and coffee mugs as the prizes.

After market hours, stay tuned for blockbuster miniseries such as advanced product seminars and Certified Financial Planning (CFP) courses. Celebrity guests, such as noted economists or congressmen, draw the best fringe-time ratings.

During the 1981 bear market, one innovative firm hired a psychologist to conduct group therapy sessions for RRs over the squawk network. When transcripts of the sessions were leaked to *The Wall Street Journal* and published in a page-one article, clients rushed to close their accounts. That brokerage firm was subsequently acquired by a major insurance company.

Every popular communications system depends upon a dynamic microphone personality to keep its ratings up. Usually a hapless junior member of the firm's research department is drafted for this slot. As emcee, he must display his wit, repartee and inside knowledge of the betting line on upcoming sporting events.

At approximately 7:30 A.M. EST the squawk networks of major firms wake up with a roll call. Although it's still an hour before the first exchange opens, early risers in the branches are eager to start the day.

As each office opens, a broker or manager yawns out its name on the network. "Midtown" (Manhattan) or "LaSalle" (Chicago) rarely get a rise, but nothing charges up sleepy speculators like the throaty roar of: *"Faaaabulous Laaaaas Veeeegas!"*

Great Moments in Squawk Box History

In one of the greatest moments in squawk box history, Sandy Weill, the CEO of Shearson Loeb Rhoades, used his firm's squawk network to tell his employees that he had agreed to sell them to American Express.

Choking back tears, he went over the benefits he saw in the merger. Everybody who listened was happy and a little bit richer—thanks to the generous purchase price paid by American Express for the company's shares.

But the general good humor in the branches broke into sentimental cheers after Sandy's dad patched into the system. He had to interrupt his son's business, he explained, just to tell him how proud of him he was.

Sometimes brokers get carried away with themselves and usurp control of a squawk network from their corporate masters.

"I remember one organized work night when the company offered a tote bag to any RR who could sell five hundred shares of Lilco within fifteen minutes," recalls one broker. "Some broker shouted out her sale just as the time period ended. She was disqualified. All of a sudden we heard brokers in twenty-seven offices around the country yelling into their boxes. They were screaming, *'Tote bag! Tote bag! Tote bag! Tote bag!'* It was like a fraternity party—with the lights out! They gave her the bag. Whoa!"

First-Year Memories

New brokers set out with ambitious goals for their first year. Industry standards call for one hundred telephone contacts a day, a sales appointment every other day, five new accounts a week and a $10,000 monthly gross commission pace by month twelve. It's a grueling experience.

But there will also be moments of joy and excitement in your first year, milestones you'll remember for the rest of your life. Opening your first account. Depositing that first client check. Getting your first company-logo coffee mug.

We asked a few veteran reps for their favorite first-year memories. Here they are:

Eating Your First Error

"I was broker of the day. An Indian woman in a sari comes walking into the office. She wants some municipal bonds. I say no problem: send me the check after you get the confirmation order. Two weeks later she hasn't paid for the trade. So I go to her house to demand payment. She looks at me and she looks at her husband and says: 'I was hypnotized.' I was determined not to pay for the error myself, so I decided to sue her. I asked a college buddy who was right out of law school to take the case. Unfortunately, he filed the suit in the wrong jurisdiction. I ended up paying the court costs too."

Meeting the CEO of Your Firm

"It was at a corporate cocktail party. My manager had sent me along for the experience. It's a good thing I had looked at the pictures in our annual report—otherwise I never would have expected that the short guy smoking a stogie was my CEO. I introduced myself by name and he stared at me belligerently. He didn't know who I was until I gave him my production number. Then I got my first Havana cigar."

First Trip to Home Office in New York

"I thought it was going to be Class A all the way, or at least better than my eighth-grade field trip. But they booked the whole class into a fleabag hotel. I was mugged and my shoes were stolen. Why would anybody want to live in that stinkpot! After one week I thanked God that a broker can make a six-figure income anywhere in America, without big-city hassles."

Your First Personal Investment

"My best client, a computer consultant, called from an airport phone. It was a quick call—he was late for his plane—but he wanted to make sure he could buy five thousand shares of a little over-the-counter software company at the opening. I figured he knew something I didn't, so I bought a thousand shares on margin myself. The client denied ever placing the call, so I ate his shares too. The company declared Chapter XI the next day.

Your First Private Office

"I started at a desk in the bullpen right under a dripping air-conditioning unit. I wanted to get out of there into my own private office, but I didn't have any seniority. Across from me was the private office of another broker, Sid Fish, who'd waste twenty minutes each morning spraying his office with Lysol while listening to the Donahue show. It was his office—but it drove me crazy. So I made a deal with my manager. If I could out-sell Fish each month for the next six months I'd get his office. He loved the idea."

Office Decorum

"The guy sitting next to me was a wild man. Every Wednesday afternoon, right before the money supply numbers, he'd go nuts. One day he whipped out a bottle of Thunderbird and guzzled it right in front of the regional manager. He got loaded and pulled a pair of panty hose over his head. After he heard the money supply number, he ran out of the office shrieking hysterically. That same guy now makes two million a year as a trader at Salomon Brothers."

A Day in the Life

6:25   Radio alarm goes off. Tuned to all-news station to catch early morning farm report.

6:35   Scrupulously attend to personal hygiene, then shower.

6:50   Watch Alan Abelson on *NBC News at Sunrise.*

6:58   Dress—for success.

7:15   During commute, listen to Og Mandino's *The Greatest Salesman in the World* book on tape.

7:59   Pick up your *Wall Street Journal* and enter the office.

8:01   Check London gold fix and U.S. stock trading in Europe.

8:02   Cheerfully greet all cage personnel by first names and offer to make them coffee.

8:05   Call ten qualified prospects. Leave urgent messages.

8:12   Read the front section of the *Wall Street Journal.*

8:30   Monitor currency openings and find out the "call" for the upcoming interest rate futures opening.

8:32   Read the second section of the *WSJ.* Turn immediately to "Heard on the Street" to see if anyone from your firm has been quoted or if any of your stocks have been mentioned.

8:35   Scan through your firm's daily recommendations for stocks, commodities and options. If any of the ideas concern any client's position you have just found an easy commission.

8:42 Ask the wire operator if any late executions from the day before were transmitted.

8:45 Then step lightly to your first trip to the rest room.

8:46—Account executives hard at work in the office library, always on the lookout for fresh money-making investment ideas.

8:47 Pour a second cup of coffee. Adjust coffee-to-milk ratio accordingly.

9:00 Watch the financial futures opening, checking if any stop or limit orders have been triggered.

9:01 Handle all client inquiries regarding financial futures opening.

9:10 Have your sales assistant cold-call fifteen prospects to see if they have any potential.

9:11 Tell the receptionist that you are going into conference and to hold all calls.

9:12   Hang out in somebody else's office to read the sports page, chat about the morning's news and discuss lunch plans.

9:30   Check the Comex gold opening.

9:35   Pick up your commission run. Assess both gross and net commissions to date. Determine if any errors occurred in yesterday's trading.

9:45   Call up the syndicate desk to find out what new issues are coming that day.

9:50   Answer client inquiries: "How's the market gonna open?"

9:58   Double-check all limit and stop-loss orders for stocks.

9:59   Make an obscene phone call to a rival broker at another firm.

10:00   Holy cow! The stock markets opened half an hour ago.

10:03   Pour yourself a third cup of coffee.

10:05   Answer client inquiries: "How'd the market open?"

10:25   Check with wire operator for any order executions.

10:30   Call any active clients who have not phoned in. Toss out a trade idea—it doesn't matter what— just to get 'em salivating.

10:50   Monitor the meat openings.

10:58   Compute commissions earned by transactions executed so far this morning and count all active orders for the day. Do you have enough action to call it a day? If not, prepare for your first appointment.

11:01   Greet client/prospect at the receptionist's desk. Say good morning to your manager as he arrives.

11:02   Profile your prospect's investment needs.

11:05   Tell him what you've got.

11:07   Sell him what he wants.

11:08   Have your sales assistant prepare all account
        agreements and collect the client's signature.
11:10   Escort client to the door, shake hands and wish
        him luck.

*11:06—A broker adjusts his personal portfolio to respond to
changing market conditions.*

11:11   Have your sales assistant call back any qualified
        prospects to schedule appointments with you.
11:13   Grab a soda from the office refrigerator, pick up
        your mail and read it in somebody else's office.
11:15   Find out what kind of commission day everybody
        is having to determine how expensive lunch should
        be.
11:25   Call up your sales assistant for a restaurant
        reservation. He or she will expect an invitation if
        you're going to a four-star expense-account
        establishment.

11:30 Walk by the cage and donate ten dollars to the back-office pizza fund.

11:31 Leave five dollars in the office DJIA pool and then proceed to lunch with your colleagues.

1:30 Call your office from the restaurant to check for messages and any order executions. If your commission quota has been achieved proceed directly to the golf course—you can play eighteen holes.

12:49—Technical analysis and apple pie: the new American business lunch.

2:50   Return to the office. Say goodbye to your manager as he leaves for the day.

3:00   Watch interest-rate futures close and place bets on the close of the S & P 500 Index.

3:02   Have your sales assistant call fifteen more prospects.

3:05   Organize a golf foursome.

3:20   Make dinner arrangements.

3:30   Read *USA Today*.

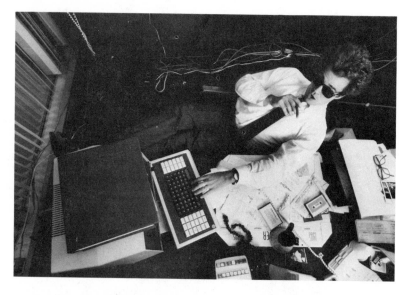

3:01—An aggressive broker scans the markets for financial opportunity. The electronic telecommunications grid is the ultimate playing field for this modern-day entrepreneurial gladiator.

3:31   Answer all client inquiries: "How's the market gonna close?"

3:56   Make sure that all stock orders have been entered by this time to insure execution.

4:00 Watch the stock market close and collect or pay off any outstanding bets.

4:01 Personally sign a stack of prospect form letters and then give them to your sales assistant to mail.

4:05 Leave for the golf course. If it's Wednesday you must wait until after the 4:12 money-supply report.

4:25—After-work relaxation must be delayed on Wednesdays until the latest money-supply numbers are released by the Fed.

CHAPTER·2

BIRTH OF A SALESMAN

Okay, so you've got a fancy job and you're legal. But if you're like many novice brokers, you're a WIMP (Woefully Intimidated Marketing Professional).

You're a WIMP because you hate calling people you don't know to sell them something they don't want. Constant rejection is the lot of the retail broker, and some new brokers can't handle it.

Terminal WIMPs panic because they think they're failures. Then they quit. It's too bad, because anyone can make it in securities sales if they grasp one simple concept: failing is the essence of selling.

That's right. All salesmen are failures. To be 100 percent successful, you have to fail 98 percent of the time. Selling is nothing more than a numbers game, and the way to win is to fail your way to success.

In this chapter, you'll learn how to turn yourself into a selling machine. It's a simple gizmo with only three moving parts: prospecting, presentation and closing. A glib, sort of friendly attitude and an utter lack of conscience are all you need to make this machine hum.

Anyone can learn to be a top salesman. If you're a child of the sixties and about to embark on your second, third, fourth or fifth career, tune in and "sell out." If you're a senior citizen looking for extra income, stop peddling your prescription drugs to minors and tap into the life savings of your fellow retirees.

Learn from the sad experience of brokers who gave up early and then watched their broker friends go on to great success. "After I quit, my own mother stopped talking to me," recalls one former broker who gave up after three months. "How could she? She was too busy talking to her broker."

Read this chapter, get to work, and you'll be headed toward the second coming of your own self-respect.

Money Talks, So Give It a Call

Before you read this section, please perform the following simple exercise (not recommended for readers with pacemakers or breast implants):

1. Extend your forefinger and raise your arm so it's parallel to the floor.
2. Turn your hand toward your chest and jab yourself sharply in the solar plexus.
3. Repeat this movement five hundred times.

No, you are not auditioning for the next Bruce Lee movie. You are preparing yourself to walk your way through one hundred phone

Telemarketing—a science anyone can learn.

numbers a day, digit by digit.

The USA has the best phone system in the world. And luckily enough for you, at any given moment most of our phones are going completely to waste, just lying there waiting to come alive.

You can rely on your firm to keep you well stocked with the phone numbers of an endless supply of possible clients. "Lead lists" are mostly filled with people who have responded to your firm's advertising campaigns and junk mail solicitations. Another standard source of prospects is names your firm buys from list companies—most typically lists of subscribers to business magazines and periodicals.

As you gain confidence, you'll quickly learn how to develop your own ways to find prospects. Prominent local businessmen and professionals are obviously at the top of your list. Keep posted on the winners of state lotteries and church bingo games for even more names of folks with cash to invest. Develop contacts and build your image by making frequent calls to local and national radio talk shows. See who's on the cover of *Time* or *Newsweek* and go for it!

The only thing a broker needs to find the money is a telephone book (but don't look under "M").

2. *Find the Unprotected Flank.* Ask an opening question. (Try "How is your net worth this morning, Mr. Smith?") Determine if your prospect is fear-motivated or greed-motivated.

3. *Intelligence Gathering.* You must now begin to record all responses on 3″ × 5″ cards. Use a top-quality felt-tip pen for smudge-free results.

Cold-Calling: Trial by Dial

Never call a new prospect without knowing exactly what you want to say and how you want to say it. Fortunately, the basic content of a good "cold call" can be reduced to the following five-step formula:

1. *The Opening.* Introduce yourself. Introduce your company. Introduce your product. Pause for a minute to make the prospect feel uncomfortable.

Cold-calling: Registered Reps of the Yukon always get their sale.

4. *First Strike*. Even if your prospect is only mildly interested, go directly for a sale at this point in the pitch. If you haven't made the prospect feel that he would be a naive loser if he turns down your offer, the answer will be no.

5. *Strategic Withdrawal*. Never offer to send information to a promising prospect. That's a cop-out for lazy, gun-shy brokers too scared to risk rejection. When you're done with the pitch, simply say thank you and then goodbye. Pound your head against your desk three times and make another call.

If you've proceeded according to plan, you're next step is the follow-up. Start by sending a note to your new prospect, enclosing a business card and an autographed 8″ × 10″ seminude glossy photo. Five days after you've sent your note, call the prospect again.

Telephone Surveillance Made Easy

"Telephone surveillance" enables RRs to systematically gather valuable background information about prospects. Using a few basic telemarketing skills, any broker can collect bulging files about a target prospect's family, personal habits and finances.

The simple genius of the technique is to call prospects when they are least likely to be in.

Begin your surveillance program by calling a prospect's home between 4 P.M. and 5:30 P.M. In most contemporary families, both the prospect and the prospect's spouse will still be commuting. If you're lucky, one or more "latchkey" children will be there to take your call. These kids are a fabulous source of uncensored information.

Follow up your chat with the kids by calling the prospect's office at lunch. Your prospect will be out, but his secretary should be in the middle of a yogurt-and-Tab desktop repast. Flirt a bit, and before you know it you'll have your prospect's Swiss bank account number.

To wrap up your telephone surveillance program, call on Sundays during NFL games and speak to the prospect's spouse for an hour or two (in the case of male prospects). If you're trying to reach a female prospect's spouse, a call timed to coincide with prime-time soaps like *Dallas* and *Dynasty* should do the trick.

Diligent pursuit of telephone surveillance turns a broker into a beloved "uncle" or "aunt" figure, a trusted friend who is asked to handle all of the family's financial affairs. You will be

Young stockbroker makes exciting discovery: Rich people live indoors.

invited to numerous bar mitzvahs and weddings. You'll even find that a couple who got to know you when they opened their first joint-IRA will turn to you when they need someone to arbitrate their divorce. Make sure you get both accounts after the split.

A word of caution. Avoid using surveillance techniques that require you to break into a prospect's home or tap into telephone company switching equipment. While these and all other methods of telephone surveillance are protected under the First Amendment, you don't want to be the first test case.

Personal Interview: Selling by Appointment Only

Sooner or later you're going to have to meet some of your clients in the flesh.

It is understandably painful for a hard-charging broker to step away from the phone during market hours, but personal meetings can help you develop a warm and lucrative relationship with clients.

You'll find that the added effort is well worth it: no laws govern the activities of consenting investors behind closed doors.

A mission to a prospect's home or office should be preceded by a moment of silence and a purification ritual of your choice. Remember not to carry any sales or promotional literature—a slim leather briefcase just large enough to hold account forms for the client's signature will suffice.

Never let the facts get in the way of your developing rapport with your client. Sell the benefit, not the product. If you're trying to sell some bonds, for example, don't talk about coupons, yields, call provisions and other esoterica.

Your seamless personal pitch can occasionally be threatened by client questions about minor technical details. If you are unable to answer a question, your credibility will be shot and you'll lose the sale. However, a devious but harmless old ruse can serve you well in such situations: call a famous "expert" to get an answer. Your client will think you have a direct line to the likes of Paul Volcker or Henry Kaufman—but the voice at the other end of the line is actually one of your office mate's doing an uncanny impersonation.

Humor always comes in handy. Be sure to memorize fifteen nonsexist, nonethnic, nonreligious, nonpolitical jokes you can tell to liven up a dull sales talk.

Seminars: The Bull Pulpit

A virtuoso violinist spends countless lonely hours fiddling with his instrument. He's richly rewarded by the glory and excitement of the concert performance. Similarly, a customer's man spends most of his time in the lonely pursuit of retail sales. But like the concert violinist, the broker can strut his stuff onstage by sponsoring seminars for the investment public.

Your first seminar may be to a handful of retirees in the basement of a nursing home. You have to start small, but keep at it. Remember, successful seminar sellers have gone on to become senators and game show hosts.

Always try to find somebody to cover the cost of putting on the seminar. You're going to need a mass

"Prosperity waits for no one . . . hop on board!"

mailing, radio spots and newspaper advertising to bring in a crowd, and these don't come cheap. Your best bet for getting some backing is to seek out investment companies actively trying to sell their products through brokers. They won't even complain if you forget to mention their product in your talk.

The basic tools of seminar selling are:

1. An extensive "qualified" prospect list that should be five times the projected attendance.

2. A handsome hand-addressed invitation with R.S.V.P. card.

3. A loyal, hardworking sales assistant.

4. A convenient seminar location, such as a hotel or Kiwanis lodge.

5. A guest speaker, preferably Henry Kissinger.

6. A single product or service to promote. The "New Ideas of the Eighties" approach doesn't work.

7. Your personal name tag, always worn on the right lapel so prospects can see your name when they shake your hand.

About a month before the big show, all seminar prospects should be contacted by phone to screen out potential assassins. If you don't have a sales assistant or secretary to make the calls, disguise your voice to avoid giving the impression that you are a low-level functionary.

Five days before the seminar date, have your sales assistant call the prospects who sent in their R.S.V.P. cards to confirm their attendance.

Early on the day of the seminar, make sure that each prospect is again reconfirmed. Have a fleet of limos ready to provide transportation for dentists and other prime prospects.

Remove any excess chairs from the seminar room or perhaps move into a smaller room at the last moment. This will require some minor adjustments in the hotel's events directory, but it will be worth the effort. Your objective is to create a crowded, smoke-filled room crammed full of qualified prospects under the influence of cheap wine and spiked cheese.

As emcee of the seminar, you shouldn't waste your opening remarks on formal introductions. Your audience expects to hear irrelevant anecdotes and ancient humor, so don't disappoint them.

Then, when you learn your noted guest speaker has either gotten drunk in transit or is hopelessly lost in the lobby, you have become the star of your own show.

What do you say? Simple! The following talk has won rave reviews from seminar-goers throughout the nation. Even if you forget what product you are touting, this presentation should book at least two straight weeks of appointments for you:

1. Discuss poetically the unlimited potential of the American people.
2. Mention why your firm is without peer in the investment industry.
3. Briefly state that you will discuss all mechani-

cal details during a Q & A session at the end of your presentation.

4. Talk about why most people are unhappy, unsatisfied, unpopular losers.

5. Make clear that users of your product or service are not like most people.

6. Signal to your assistant to lock all the doors to the seminar room, even if he or she is lying unconscious and partially nude in the back row.

7. Plunge into the crowd immediately when you're done, doing away with the promised question period. Touch the people. Let them touch you.

Don't be afraid of their love!

8. Work the crowd with a uniform greeting as you move about the room. "Hey, fella," was Nelson Rockefeller's trademark; try "sir" and "ma'am."

9. After making personal contact with everyone in the room, wash your hands and leave.

Do not succumb to the open bar; get in a cab and head for the airport. Don't come back for a week. In the interim your sales assistant will have booked appointments with everyone who attended the seminar.

Client Extinction: Be a Darwinner

The basic sales techniques are all a newly registered rep needs to build a good client book. But even if you're already driving a Ferrari, you can't afford to stop searching for new and better clients.

For one thing, you will lose many of the clients

you worked so hard to get. Stress-related diseases, sudden changes in the market environment and unfair competition from banks all cause steady client attrition.

This weeding out of the weak investors in your client book should be welcomed. Indeed, a good broker seeks to accelerate the natural evolutionary process of client extinction by routinely purging the weak from his client roster. Brokers who don't get rid of their inferior clients themselves become inferior. Eventually, such brokers end up devoting all their time to babbling about the economy to worthless clients who have no intention of investing any money.

It's easy to spot a client who belongs on your endangered-client list. A particularly common genus is the "coupon clipper," a fickle and demanding beast who whiles away time by talking to brokers instead of by watching TV. Almost as bad when it comes to generating

Direct mail: It worked then. It works now. It will always work. (Source: Smithsonian Institution)

commissions is the "fully invested" client, an investor happy to hold on to a conservative portfolio. A final and potentially hostile creature is the "discontented" client, a client who has lost a great deal of money. Some discontents blame you. Others blame themselves. All have lost their craving to make self-destructive lunges toward millions.

Each of the above client species should be allowed to recede into the primordial ooze whence they came. If a client doesn't make the grade, cancel his Christmas card and sell his name to Publishers Clearing House.

Tossing away clients like so many old socks is pleasant, but you have to remember that each client you terminate must be replaced. Bigger and better clients are the only means of securing a bigger income.

That's why you are now ready to learn the secrets of Advanced Marketing Techniques.

Advanced Marketing Techniques

Finding big money used to be easy. A customer's man would simply join a country club, the local opera society and a few nonsensical, do-gooder organizations and he would be rubbing elbows with the elite.

In today's faster-paced society, making connections with the rich and powerful isn't so easy. "I became a notary public and put a sign out in front of my apartment, figuring that movers and shakers would drop in to have important documents notarized," recalls one Ohio investment professional. "But the only thing that's come out of it so far was a coffee klatch with Vice President George Bush and his lovely wife, Barbara."

Halfway measures won't do when you're in pursuit of the big bucks. But there's an easy way to find the clients you need. All you have to know is this one basic rule:

NEVER GET TO KNOW ANYBODY WHO ISN'T RICHER THAN YOU ARE.

The Strategic Vacation

Advanced Marketing Technique No. 1 is perhaps the most pleasant selling program you'll find in the brokerage trade: the strategic vacation. This potent marketing gambit moves your prospecting operation out to the glamorous resorts and vacation hot spots favored by the world's rich.

But don't be seduced by the hedonistic implications of this potent selling strategy. Keep your wits about you as you "leverage your exposure" in style. In fact, a sober, calculated approach to your strategic vacation should yield you a highly qualified client every eight waking hours.

You can pick your strategic vacation spot by scanning the pages of *People*, the *National Enquirer*, and transcripts of *Lifestyles of the Rich and Famous*. Avoid exotic settings favored by the bohemian set and other offbeat locales populated by the younger, upwardly mobile types look-ing for unspoiled native charm. If you're out selling tax shelters, the last thing you need is to get machine-gunned by revolutionaries on the golf course.

Don't forget that what you're after is money. Oil money, trust-fund money, rock-and-roll money—it doesn't matter, just so long as it's big money. You'll know you've chosen wisely when the production crew of the next James Bond movie rolls into town.

Begin your prospecting as soon as you arrive by sharing a cab or rickshaw with prosperous-looking arrivés. You may find that this works so well, you'll spend ten days shuttling back and forth.

At the resort or hotel— from the dining room to the disco—the wealthy guests are sitting ducks because of the soothing effects of suntan oil, large meals and imbibition.

Be careful to avoid members of the nouveau riche who have taken out second mortgages to afford their ten days in the sun. You can steer clear of an under-capitalized prospect by discreetly obtaining the carbons of his credit card receipts. Use your portable computer to tap into the card issuer's data bank.

Whatever you do, don't worry about coming off like some kind of "con artist." Freely admit that you are a "money manager" or an "investment adviser." Once someone shows a modicum of interest, you're ready for the kill. Pull the trigger. Then pull it again.

An aggressive salesman may not be content with the simple "getting to know you" approach. If you're really ambitious, here are a few tricks:

☐ *Disguising yourself as a bellhop.* This disguise can put you into intimate situations that can be turned into selling opportunities.
☐ *Posing as an athletic "pro."* All you have to do is shell out a few bucks for flashy sports attire. Under no circumstances let this ruse force you into actually engaging in athletic activity.
☐ *Playing your cards right.* Vacation spots with gambling casinos offer an ideal opportunity to get in with "high rollers." You'll make the right connections by gambling big bucks in a conspicuous, attention-grabbing way. All you need to know are a few risk-free tricks to prevent traumatic losses. When the dealer isn't looking, substitute loaded dice for the house dice if you're playing craps. At roulette, little magnets cleverly hidden under the table do the trick.

We'll send you on your way with a final important reminder:

Never, never forget that you're working full-time on this vacation. "Sailors on leave" is not the proper theme for a strategic vacation.

Belly Up to the Big Time: The Art of Raising Equity at a Bar

Perhaps the most venerable and time-tested of all Advanced Marketing Techniques is the great art of raising equity in a bar.*

Seasoned practitioners of this great art form usually gross in excess of $250,000. But because of extremely high personal overhead for alimony and child support, these artists typically do not have a great deal of discretionary income to spend on purely libidinous activities. It's not a craft that should be trifled with by the novice.

Be selective—because if you find the right bar it can become your personal branch office, with convenient hours, an independent support staff and an unauditable PR budget that can profitably be cross-fertilized with a company-supplied expense account. Avoid establishments with exotic dancers, free "buffalo wing" hors d'oeuvres or with three or more souped-up Harley Davidsons parked out front.

Before you unwind and loosen up, indulge in a little independent advertising. Slow starters can post their business cards in the restrooms and at the pay phones. Graffiti might seem more permanent, but people really do enjoy the personal touch that a fresh business card provides. Insert your card in the pockets of each

*Women brokers may be on equal footing with their male colleagues battling for new accounts in the board room, on the tennis court, or at a sales seminar, but when the action shifts downstairs to the barroom, they are definitely interlopers. That's right, the last bastion of male supremacy in finance is neither in the executive suite nor on the trading room floor. It's not in private clubs, professional associations, or even gymnasiums. It's behind the swinging doors of a saloon. This is no sexist gibe at the drinking ability of women brokers. It is a simple observation of fact that can yield important insights into marketing financial services successfully.

patron's outer garment by bribing the coat-check concessionaire. Finally, deposit napkins with hand-printed investment strategies scribbled on them at each table. This will impress sophisticated investors who know that some of the greatest economic and financial ideas of this century were first conceived on cocktail napkins (the Laffer curve, the debenture and the outline for *The Official Stockbroker's Handbook* immediately leap to mind).

Even stock market pros sometimes put themselves in impossible barroom jams. A producer at work at a bar cannot avoid angry confrontations with clients who have lost large sums of money in ill-advised market plays. There is no hold button on your bar seat. Faced with the possibility of a nasty scene a broker has only one option: he must quickly incapacitate the client. A swift knee to the groin followed instantly with a Heimlich maneuver

COMRADE BROKER?

MOSCOW—A mustachioed man wearing a tattered old Soviet Army field coat stands suspiciously amid the bustle of a crowded downtown street corner.

He approaches a passing American journalist. He pulls open his coat, revealing a crudely fabricated pinstripe suit, a poor match with his thick-soled imitation cordovan wing tips.

"Hey, guy!" the man says quietly. "I give you big dollars for any stock certificate, debenture or soy bean contract."

The journalist—who cannot be identified here for national security reasons—had come to this corner with five pairs of Levi's button-flap, prewashed jeans and a briefcase full of Abba (a popular Swedish rock group) tapes to cover just this contingency.

Such merchandise could normally command enough rubles to keep a Minsk family in cabbage for a lifetime. Not here. "Catch you later, pig. Jeans make lousy inflation hedge," the street-corner entrepreneur sneered. "Abba no longer quoted on Pinsk over-the-counter market."

This recent street-corner encounter reveals in a classic *Wall Street Journal*–style microcosm a surprising new wrinkle in the Soviet Union's dissident movement: stockbrokers.

Throughout this vast, godless land, thousands of idealistic free thinkers have joined underground networks of stockbrokers despite the threat of harsh KGB regulatory intervention. (It is no coincidence that Soviet negotiators harshly rejected U.S. proposals to include the right to "free and unfettered trading of marketable securities" during the Helsinki human rights negotiations.) Officials at the Voice of America report that its radio broadcasts of "Wall Street Week" in fifteen of the languages spoken behind the Iron Curtain have become its most popular show. In some parts of Moscow, a new *samizdat* publication that contains only mimeographed copies of The Standard & Poor's Stock Guide and The Value Line Investment Survey is passed eagerly from hand to hand.

On a recent Saturday evening, a French diplomat walking down a street in Leningrad was stunned when he was hit on the head by a water balloon thrown from an upstairs window. Going up to investigate, the envoy found a tiny apartment filled with dissidents reenacting a typical Merrill Lynch sales incentive meeting. "We love America and
(continued on page 257)

to camouflage the assault gets the job done.

Walking into the office at the crack of noon with a handful of orders closed the night before is the reward for expert practitioners of "pub-ic" offerings. Looking around at your buddies who are prisoners of time is a gleeful experience. But it is the money that really makes all the discipline and sacrifice worthwhile. Big bucks, gross commissions, unlimited income is what it is all about.

You Got to Believe

Perhaps the most unpleasant bureaucratic tradition in the brokerage business is the sales meeting, the adult equivalent of high school study hall.

Reps get "invited" to sales meeting when their monthly gross falls below an arbitrary managerial target. At some firms these deadly affairs take place as frequently as once a week.

Managers don't like sales meetings any more than brokers do, but they are required to run them by top management. Thus these get-togethers are even worse than they have to be.

Sales meetings are scheduled at 8:00 A.M. Monday morning or Friday night after the markets close, depending on how vindictive your manager feels. If you're lucky, the sales meeting will consist of a presentation from a desperate tax-shelter packager or mutual-fund representative. The worst scenario is when the manager has to run the meeting himself—a man bitter about giving up his racquetball time can be merciless.

An edge of terror is essential to successful sales meetings. Like time wasted in high schools or prisons, unavoidable boredom must be tempered by danger.

To keep brokers properly nervous, managers often

use sales meetings as an opportunity to deliver bad news. A classic case was when Merrill Lynch developed an elaborate ruse to perpetrate a broker blood-bath.

It began as a "bear market practice" for the mid-Atlantic offices. All "qualifying" brokers were requested to attend. A typical snorer, except for the presence of a regional v.p. who announced that the branch would close and that each broker had been reassigned to a nearby office.

After the meeting, each rep discovered an envelope on his desk. In it was either a map showing directions to his new office or a pink slip. Over thirty percent of the brokers were terminated.

Attending sales meetings is humiliating and meant to stay that way.

THE FIVE MOST POPULAR CLIENT EXCUSES AND HOW TO OVERCOME THEM

1. "Gee, it sounds great, but I've got to talk to my wife/husband before giving you any money."

☐ "Do you think Boone Pickens clears everything with his wife? You've got to move fast to make money, especially with the kind of sizzling inside information we're talking about here."

2. "I didn't get the information you said you'd mail me."

☐ "Sir, you did get the message. Our federal government's service infrastructure is corrupt and on the verge of collapse. If they can't deliver the mail now, hyperinflation is inevitable by '89."

3. "I've already got a good broker and a solid cash management account at Merrill Lynch."

☐ "Well then, I've called you just in time. My firm acquired Merrill Lynch an hour ago, and we've discovered that they put all their CMA funds in a lira check-kiting scheme. I'm afraid you're the victim of a terrible hoax."

4. "I don't have any money—it's all tied up in real estate."

☐ "That's too bad. Yesterday's financial hedge is today's financial weed. How about a wraparound second mortgage to pick up some leverage and put a little green stuff into your pocket? Rates can't hold at 25 percent forever, you know."

5. "I sure could use some financial planning. I was laid off at the plant. . ."

☐ [Click.]

The Plane Truth

You'd think that two hundred people 15,000 feet above the ground flying at six hundred miles an hour in an aerodynamic toothpaste tube would be a captive audience eager to hear about the benefits of financial services.

Sadly, planes are not a good place to prospect.

With the possible exceptions of the Concorde, wealthy Americans cannot be found aboard commercial airliners. Your best prospects—corporate leaders and the entrepreneurial elite—travel strictly in small private aircraft.

When flying on a scheduled airline, it's much safer to travel heavily sedated. If you remain conscious, you will undoubtedly embarrass yourself by talking about payout rates and bogus product developments to the executive sitting next to

"Were all the customer's men in the country laid end to end—it would be a very good thing for the country."

—John A. Straley, an early editor of *The Bawl Street Journal*

"Great names, big talk, marble and mahogany, and poor excuses have failed us."

—An investor in a letter to his son in the early thirties

"The public's favorite picture of stockbrokers at their trade seems to be that of an abattoir that makes a specialty of lambs."

—Gustave A. Lefebvre

you. You will later learn that your companion is a broker for a competing financial services organization.

At the airport, sales opportunities are even fewer. Airports are just bus stations where the depraved rabble walk fast and wear business suits or torn panty hose.

However, be sure to join some of the prestigious first-class airline clubs. The clubs have sumptuous lounges offering comfortable work space, coffee and telephones.

If you're into grandstanding, a broker can prospect by dominating the club telephone and speaking loudly and incessantly about prices into the receiver. This quickly leads into giving quotes to travelers seated near the phone and then to executing trades from these spontaneous customers.

Airports and airlines are not demographically rich spawning grounds for monster clients. Your time would be better spent giving investment seminars on cruise ships.

Last-Ditch Selling Techniques: Appear to Be Weak and Pathetic

Sometimes turning on the charm simply doesn't work. If there's a gruesome bear market on and all people want to buy is canned goods to store in their basement, you have to consider drastic methods if you want to earn a nice living.

An effective and time-tested last-ditch strategy is to present yourself as weak, pathetic or, if all else fails, physically and mentally handicapped. Masquerading as an abject social reject often elicits the sympathy and charity of potential investors.

In telephone sales, an uncontrollable speech impediment not only limits your sales pitch to three words but breaks the heart of a prospect who would otherwise hang up on you. Sometimes a phony foreign accent suggesting recent immigration via rowboat through shark-infested waters touches a responsive chord. A third but considerably more subtle approach is to give the impression that you're a suicidally depressed loser on the verge of "ending it all."

For face-to-face meetings, you can use commercially available props to create the right image. Hooks, wheelchairs, crutches and portable dialysis machines all make dandy sales aids. If you're on a tight budget, a pair of dark sunglasses and a cane will work just fine.

CHAPTER · 3

PRODUCT, OR, WHAT'S ON THE SHELF OF THE FINANCIAL SUPERMARKET?

Let's begin our plunge into the world of financial products with a fable, a tale of two brokers, Bill and Betty.

Bill and Betty both work for the same brokerage firm. Bill sells futures. Betty sells tax shelters.

Both are in their mid-thirties. Both earn six-figure incomes. Both floss after every meal, even in restaurants.

Bill spends all day on the phone, talking to clients and barking rapid-fire instructions to his firm's pit brokers on the floor of the Chicago commodities ex-

changes. Bill never leaves the office during trading hours. Lunch means a couple of Twinkies and his tenth cup of coffee.

Betty rarely uses the Quotron machine on her desk. She frequently leaves the office, often for expensive lunches with wealthy clients or their lawyers and accountants. Betty often goes out of town on all-expenses-paid junkets to visit the oil wells and Sun Belt apartment complexes that absorb much of the tax-shelter money she raises.

Bill is a risk taker. Betty is a risk avoider. Bill spends a fortune on psychotherapy and Valium. Betty spends it on Dale Carnegie motivational tapes and tofu milkshake binges.

Bill will probably die in his early fifties, a victim of stress. Betty will die of gunshot wounds sustained during a convenience store holdup.

There may be no justice, but there is truth in this short little story. In the brokerage industry, you are what you sell. The product you pitch determines the life you live, the people you meet, the time you get up in the morning and what you eat for dinner.

The Only Thing All Financial Products Have in Common Is Commissions

This chapter is all about products, but unlike any other financial reference source, it is written from the viewpoint of the seller. You'll find it free of jargon, cumbersome facts and fancy mathematical calculations.

We have surveyed all of the major products sold by today's retail stockbrokers with one key consideration in mind. It's a rule followed by all of today's top producers. It is the essence of what we call "product knowledge." So get out your yellow-tip Magic Marker, because this is the only thing you'll need to underline in the entire book:

HOW MUCH MONEY YOU MAKE DEPENDS ON WHAT YOU SELL AND HOW OFTEN YOU SELL IT.

If you want to succeed in the business, you must take control of the products you sell. Letting your firm or your clients tell you what to sell is the surest guarantee of a mediocre career.

Your overriding priority is to pick the right mix of high-commission products. Sometimes that means selling a range of profitable products; sometimes that means selling just one product. The more you sell, the more money you will make. The more money you make, the more successful you will appear. And success breeds success.

Sadly, the image projected by some major brokerage firms deliberately obscures the entrepreneurial imperative that is the core of their business. For some reason the brutally aggressive financial arena has been dubbed "the financial supermarket." Smart brokers reject this passive image. They have no desire to become pin-striped checkout clerks making the minimum wage.

Like many indoor employees who do no heavy lifting, brokers get paid by commission. Each time a broker sells a product, he generates what's known as a "gross commission" for his firm. After the firm squanders most of the money on overhead, legal fees and senior executive bonuses, the broker gets his share, or "net commission." (When brokers talk shop, and refer to "production" they are talking about gross commissions, the measure of a broker's selling prowess.)

The net commissions a broker receives vary depending on the product he sells and the firm he works for. Payout schedules are complicated and jealously guarded by brokerage firms. All brokers strive for a regular payout that approaches 50 percent. No firm will ever allow them to keep more.*

Product mix and gross production levels determine payout. Sales credits from agency transactions (stock or option trades sent to the

*In fact, the recent industry trend is to reduce payouts for all but the highest-grossing brokers.

"The Curse of Calamari."

Just when you thought it was safe to go into the water.

floor of an exchange for execution) have a sliding rate from 25 percent to 45 percent plus. Bonds and over-the-counter stocks that are marked up and sold from your firm's inventory (a principal transaction) net a broker 40 percent or more. So-called "packaged products" like mutual funds and tax shelters generally pay 45 percent to 50 percent.

Options and futures are the most profitable products because of the natural propensity for client dollars invested in these vehicles to turn over rapidly. This is a natural side effect of the price volatility of highly leveraged investments and is *not* caused by "churning," an expression used to describe excessive transactions in an account. Account churning is an immoral act that all registered representatives abhor and condemn.

New commission-rich products will always be moving down Wall Street's fashion-conscious runway to keep things interesting. But you can't be a product hopper forever. The sooner you successfully specialize your selling efforts, the sooner you'll get rich. Amazingly enough, the affluence you achieve through successful selling will become a symbol of your investment acumen to clients and prospects.

We hope the following Encyclopedia of Financial Products will take some of the pain out of finding your way in the financial services business.

The Encyclopedia of Financial Products

Fed Tightening Moves Ease Inflation Fears, Bond Yields Drop

Restrictive Fed Actions Linked to Rise in Bond Yields

Bonds and Other "Fixed-Income Securities"

Welcome to the wacky, zany world of bonds.

Daily speculation about Federal Reserve monetary policy and market reactions to the proclamations of Wall Street financial pundits keep this market hopping. Add to that the all-American pastime of Deficit Mania, and a smart broker can turn his cli-ent's bond holdings into a high-velocity trading platform.

Topping your list of ripe clients should be conservatives who like to rail endlessly about government spending. These public-spirited citizens hungrily snap up the latest U.S. Treasury issues, happy to get revenge against the fiscally irresponsible folks in Washington.

You may still run into a

few clients interested in holding bonds for income and safety, the traditional appeal of most bonds. You won't have any trouble giving them what they want because of the vast array of "fixed-income securities" that go far beyond the familiar U.S. Treasury issues. Zero coupons, Euros, floating-rate notes, mortgage-backed securities are all investments with added sizzle to investors.

What's the commission?

From $7.50 to $50.00 or more on each thousand-dollar increment in face value.

Huh?

The yield curve (the relationship between the yields and maturities of bonds) is the yellow brick road for sales commissions in debt securities. The farther out in time a security matures, the bigger the sales credit for the broker. For this reason most retail brokers concentrate on "term" bonds, bonds that mature in fifteen to thirty years. One dollar of client equity should yield the broker at least six cents in commissions a year, no matter what the mix of "munie," "guvie," or "corporate bonds" in the account. Because of the spectacular leverage possible with U.S. Treasury bonds (a dime on the dollar), "guvies" are popular trading vehicles. Using this leverage should generate commissions two to eight times greater than bonds in a cash account.

Bonds that are deemed risky pay higher commissions than low-risk bonds (and also generate more income to investors). Two credit agencies take the guesswork out of risk analysis for bond hawkers. Standard & Poor's and Moody's rate the credit worthiness of all debt issuers willing to submit their balance sheets to scrutiny. "AAA" is the strongest rating granted, though many issuers successfully sell their debt without a rating, including the U.S. government.

Whom should I sell bonds to?

Almost anybody who has saved some money will be interested in the potential return on their capital in the tax-free municipal, or state tax-free government market. Your prime prospect is anybody over the age of forty-five who has not been diagnosed as having a terminal illness.

It sounds like bonds would be a good prospecting tool, eh?

One of the best. If you happen to call somebody who has some money lying around, a municipal bond investment is an easy sell. These routine sales will pay for your prospecting time. You can add zest to your sales pitch by heralding new underwritings. This is key, because commissions on underwritings are richer than those in the secondary market. Another bonus for brokers at large firms is that, because of this constant stream of underwritings, your firm will undoubtedly accumulate sizable "unsold" positions. This inventory has got to be moved. Retail brokers may not give a hoot about how much capital their firm ties up in bond inventories, but credits can become very, very attractive on inventory that has been parked on the shelf too long.

As a broker, what is my upside? Downside? Legal exposure?

The upside is a solid commission stream flowing from a stable account base. Even when market declines tear into the current value of client bond portfolios, brokers can take heart. Losses can be turned into additional trades by swapping the depreciated bonds for similar issues, generating valuable tax losses. Brokers who sell bonds for a living can be proud that the finest minds in finance are on their team, working behind the scenes at new ways to package debt. Reading about these developments in between sales will amuse debt brokers while everyone else in the office is glued to their Quotron machines watching the DJIA.

As to the downside, it takes years of prospecting and accumulating "house accounts" before the commission stream on a pure bond book will reach flood levels. Therefore it is wise to work for a firm with an aggressive product/broker advertising plan, although it may mean paying for newspaper ads out of your own pocket. Without the prospects generated by advertising a broker cannot pierce the six-digit income level. Newspaper ads are most effective, especially when placed in the local business pages next to bank advertisements for CDs and other money-market accounts. Bonds work in this environment because they are simple investments that can be sold with one number—yield.

Legal exposure? If nobody in America can agree on the direction of interest rates, who is going to hold a few bond losses against a salesperson? However, the use of advertising does bring you exposure on a number of fronts. The Federal Trade Commission and NASD have guidelines that you and your firm have to follow regarding the submission of ad copy to the NASD and proof that bonds advertised are in inventory. Bait and switch is as tough in bonds as it is in refrigerators.

What firms market bonds?

There is no shortage of product. Any registered rep at any firm can sell bonds.

Financial Planning

Do you want to be the Mr. Whipple of the financial supermarket? If so, give financial planning a squeeze.

Financial planning allows you to take benevolent control of a client's entire financial life, putting you in charge of all money decisions ranging from insurance to tax avoidance. Your clients will enjoy the comfort of believing that they

have gained access to the kind of sophisticated financial and investment advice once only available to the former wives of Johnny Carson.

To earn the official designation of certified financial planner (CFP), all you have to do is complete a one-year correspondence course. It's easier and more profitable than any of the opportunities advertised on most matchbooks.

What's the commission?

Financial planning *means* big commissions, even though financial planning itself is not a commissionable product. Instead, it is a conceptual sales approach revolving around high-commission products like insurance and tax shelters.

So how does it affect my bottom line?

Financial planning not only increases your business

in high-commission products, but it also dramatically boosts your percentage participation in your clients' disposable income and savings. What's more, the package products your clients buy do not have prices reported in the financial section of the paper or anywhere else. This reinforces the client's reliance on his personal investment guru (you). The client may emerge somewhat poorer, but you've provided him with a service: a panic-free state of mind.

Is it a good prospecting tool?

Servicing clients rather than prospecting takes up most of a CFP's time. That means that a planner must organize a steady and efficient prospecting campaign that is not time-intensive. Veteran CFPs recommend: (1) a seminar once a quarter;

(2) small newspaper ads in the real estate section for tax-sheltered investments; (3) continuing direct-mail programs; (4) a personal listing in the phone book under FINANCIAL PLANNING, an absolute must for the serious CFP; (5) granting frequent interviews to *Money* magazine.

As a broker, what is my upside? My downside?

The upside is enjoying a six-figure income as an expert in tax and money matters. You can enjoy a feeling of superiority over your CPA and tax lawyer friends, who had to endure grueling professional training, only to submit to the humiliating servitude of hourly billing. Even the shiest and most ineffectual broker can hide under the camouflage of a one-year certificate CFP course to successfully become an expert ministering to the needs of shell-shocked investors.

The downside is your inevitable absorption into the financial services firm of the future as a salaried equity raiser, giving your accountant and lawyer friends the last laugh. The financial services industry first started pushing financial planning as a fancy gimmick to revive battered brokers during bear markets. About the same time, independent insurance agents also began to enter the planning field in a desperate attempt to garner some semblance of respect. With such inauspicious beginnings, there's a chance that brokers in financial planning will have to move to a single fee or hourly billing system, a gilded cage for anyone driven by the excitement of commission sales.

What legal trouble can a CFP get into?

To find out, refer to the insurance, tax-shelter and mutual-fund sections of The Encyclopedia of Financial Products.

Corporate Finance

Yes, a lowly retail broker can dabble in the tony and glamorous business of corporate finance.

Even if you work for a major national securities firm with a New York investment banking department crammed with overpaid Ivy League MBAs, you can horn in on some corporate deals.

What do you have that they don't? No matter where you're based, if you're a successful retail broker you have many clients who need corporate finance services. Entrepreneurs, executives, and members of local water and sewer boards live and work on Main Street, and you are their stockbroker. You're in a perfect position to sniff out opportunities for new financings and for prospective mergers and acquisitions.

Don't let the corporate finance drones scare you away with MBA doubletalk. The skills of your firm's corporate finance department are just another product that you can offer qualified clients.

So what's the payout for bringing a deal to my firm?

Anywhere from a flat $10,000 to 50 percent of your firm's take on the deal.

That could be an enormous amount of money. But can I make a steady living at it?

We're not talking steady living. We're talking windfall profits. Treat your foray into corporate finance as an occasional lark, but don't let it go to your head.

As a broker, what is my upside? Downside? Legal exposure?

The rewards for lassoing a deal go well beyond the initial finder's fee. If your matchmaking results in a new stock or bond issue, a limited partnership offering or any other kind of product, your firm should send the clients to you. Your

WALL STREET GOES HOLLYWOOD

Wall Street not only raises money to finance films, but also sometimes makes money at the box office. Over the years, finance has served as a vehicle for a surprising number of movies. These movies may have come and gone, like so many stock market cycles, but they remain a fascinating glimpse at the changing image of stockbrokers over the years.

1. *Stock Exchange*
Producer unknown. (191?)

2. *The Night of the Pub*
The Pub is a broker's clerk who stands up to his boss to save face in his neighborhood.

Double Indemnity: *Financial planner Fred MacMurray devising a comprehensive investment and insurance package for Barbara Stanwyck.*

Mr. Skeffington: *Wealthy stockbroker ties the knot with Bette Davis.*

He ends up with a promotion. Starring Billy Truex. (1920)

3. *The Confidence Man*

Oil stock promoters swindle an old miser in a small town. Starring Thomas Meighan. (1924)

4. *Stocks and Blondes*

A Wall Street romance. Young broker falls for a nightclub dancer. She teaches him about life and he almost loses his job. Starring Gertrude Astor, Jacqueline Logan, Richard Gallagher and Albert Conti. (1928)

5. *Wall Street*

Roller McCray—a ruthless financier—is squeezing a rival broker named Tabor. Tabor's wife snubs McCray in a posh restaurant. The social putdown inspires McCray to ruin Tabor. Tabor commits suicide, and a repentant McCray offers his profits to Mrs. Tabor. She uses the money to squeeze him. Ruined, he falls in love with the widow and eventually marries her. Starring Aileen Pringle, Ralph Ince, Sam De Grasse, Phillip Strange,

Earnest Hilliard, Jimmy Finlayson, Freddie Burke Fredericks. (1929)

6. *We're Rich Again*

A once affluent family seeks to marry their daughter off to a wealthy stockbroker—while simultaneously dodging bill collectors. Starring Buster Crabbe, Edna May Oliver. (1934)

7. *You Can't Take It With You*

Lionel Barrymore plays Grandpa Vanderhoff, an eccentric old coot who raises his family to enjoy life. His granddaughter falls for a young customer's man. The freedom of the Vanderhoff household fascinates the young man as he starts to wean himself from Wall Street and his father's firm. Based on the Kaufman and Hart play. Also starring James Stewart and Edward Arnold. (1938)

8. *Johnny Apollo*

Edward Arnold is a convicted Wall Street broker whose fashionable friends forsake him. His son, played by Tyrone Power, is a spoiled college boy who turns his back on finance and becomes a gangster for philosophical reasons. (1940)

9. *Here Comes Mr. Jordan*

Robert Montgomery is a boxer whose soul is prematurely snatched by an overanxious angel. The angel, remorseful about his fateful mixup, agrees to let Montgom-

You Can't Take It With You: *Have you hugged your registered representative today?*

ery live out his time in another man's body. Montgomery assumes the body and life of a ruthless Wall Street banker—but he gets his girl and wins the world boxing championship anyway. (1941)

10. *Double Indemnity*

Fred MacMurray plays a financial planner cum insurance salesman who devises a comprehensive plan for a steamy gold digger's investment and insurance needs. He gets involved in murder and insurance fraud, but manages to shake off the stress by bowling and remembering that "the customer is always right." Also starring Barbara Stanwyck and Edward G. Robinson. (1944)

11. *Mr. Skeffington*

Bette Davis plays a vain social climber who marries Claude Rains—a wealthy stockbroker—for money. As she ages, Davis comes to realize that a woman is only beautiful when she is loved. A great tearjerker with a subtle subplot about anti-Semitism. (1944)

12. *From the Terrace*

The ultimate story of Wall Street ambition, based on John O'Hara's novel. Paul Newman plays the resentful son of a Pennsylvania steel man. Newman has grand ambitions that he thinks he can better realize as a playboy in New York society. Living in NYC he marries well—but is cut out of equity ownership in an aircraft company he and a wealthy war buddy organize. Coincidentally, he saves the grandson of a Wall Street patriarch and is brought into the brokerage business. He risks his partnership when he decides to divorce his cold, snobby wife. Fantastic! (1960)

13. *The Marriage of a Young Stockbroker*

Richard Benjamin likes to watch. This movie is every registered reps favorite cult film about modern customer's men. Benjamin plays a voyeuristic young broker whose peculiar obsession causes his marriage to fall apart. A must see! (1971)

From the Terrace: *Paul Newman severely underdressed for an important sales presentation.*

14. *Rollover*

As an oversheltered oil heiress, Jane Fonda proves an easy mark for Kris Kristofferson's deal-hungry investment banker. A proxy fight and plans for a merger spree suffice for heavy foreplay in PG-rated sex scenes. Unfortunately, a plan by Arabs to liquidate all their dollar assets and buy gold destroys the economies of the free world. This might ruin the day of an average Wall Street man, but it takes the kinks out of Fonda and Kristofferson's relationship. (1981)

15. *Wanda Whips Wall Street*

XXX feature starring Veronica Hart as Wanda, an ambitious young RR who stages a "pink-mail" raid on a Wall Street brokerage firm. Her sexual takeover attempt is foiled only at the last moment by a well-connected private eye. Also starring Tish Ambrose, Samantha Fox, Jamie Gillis, and Ron Jeremy. (1982)

16. *Trading Places*

The Duke Brothers—old-line commodity brokers from Philadelphia—make a wager about the importance of heredity versus environment in human behavior. The two brothers ruin the life of their young trader—Dan Aykroyd —and replace him with Eddie Murphy—a derelict street hustler. Though this switch was done in the interest of science and a one-dollar bet, Murphy and Aykroyd team up for revenge. The climax occurs on the floor of the New York Mercantile Exchange in the Frozen Orange Juice pit. (1983)

gross from the sell side of the deal could exceed the finder's fee. You never dreamed there could be such a nice view from the ground floor.

The downside is the potential destruction of your brokerage business as selling and client service time are sacrificed for your big-ticket safari.

Legal exposure? Deal making occurs in an amoral vacuum. Don't worry about the law, worry about the lawyers. When they stick their fingers in the pie, watch out.

MBAs love fancy talk. Will buzzwords help wire a deal?

Mum's the word. Don't let your office manager know what you are up to or he will cut your deal short out of pure malice.

Equities: Honk If You Love Value

Every night without fail the network news shows pitch the stock market to America. No matter how bad the news, the Dow Jones Industrials always get their due.

With PR like that, it's no wonder that many people still equate investing with stocks.

But people buy equities not only because they've been brainwashed by the Eastern media establishment. For one thing, stocks have sexy-sounding names and symbols—no high-flying computer company would call itself Acme Computer or AAA Electronics. Shareholders are not neglected by the companies they invest in: they receive attractively designed share certificates and lots of mail full of facts, figures and four-color glossy photographs (anything to keep the shareholders from making it to the footnotes). Best of all, when a dividend check comes in the mail, your clients will praise you for putting them in a position of finally getting a "rebate" from a company to make up for all the shoddy products they've been sold in the past.

What's the commission?

Commission rates range from one percent to two percent of the total purchase price, depending on the number of shares transacted. So-called discount brokers—the slave ships of the financial services industry—advertise comparative rates every day, while you're out trying to earn a living.

Can you be more specific? How much can I squeeze out of one dollar in client equity each year?

A broker can expect to earn from two to six cents on a dollar of client equity, depending on turnover and how effective the broker is in getting clients to leverage their investment by buying on margin. Active stock traders can substantially alter the average— sometimes one monster client is all a broker can handle. A first-year rep interested in building a classic stockbroker's portfolio should have opened two hundred equity accounts with an average market value of $10,000. Hitting the two-million-dollar mark puts a broker on the threshold of big production . . . a classic beginning.

Sounds like hard work. Whom do I sell stocks to?

Anybody who answers the phone.

Is it a good prospecting tool?

Yes and no. It depends on the type of stock jockey you want to be. If, like so many others, you've decided to offer full service for the full commissions charged, prospecting for stock business might prove to be an administrative nightmare. Service brokers provide their clients with reams of information, almost all in the form of photocopied sheets from the *Standard & Poor's* Stock Guide, *Value Line* and other investment services. Imagine having to go through an elaborate song and dance with every prospect you call (there are only so many times a sane person can recap last week's *Wall Street Week*). If delivering this kind of service is your game, stick to municipal bonds or tax shelters when you're prospecting.

If you're really serious about selling stocks, though, forget about service and prospect away. Your goal is to build large positions in a handful of target stocks, so you have to get lots of new business. But you won't do it with photocopied data sheets. *You sell by telling stories.* A "position broker" is a commission-earning descendant of Homer, a paragon of the oral tradition.

Say what?

A position broker peddles stocks by telling stories that grab the imagination of the investing public. You don't have to say anything new, but you must know how to relate a simple yarn of business opportunity, not cluttered with market jargon and confusing numbers. You can choose from among seven Great Stock Themes. Each touches a subcon-

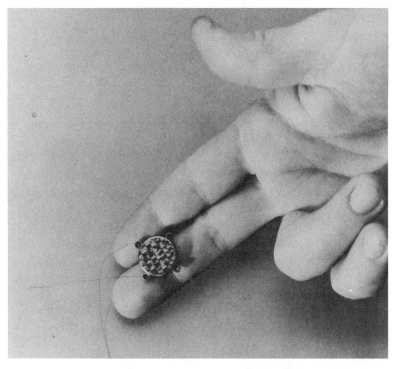

The edible microchip: the only cure for a high-tech hangover.

scious nerve in a prospect, compelling the sucker to blurt out, "I see, it's another IBM."

Okay, tell me a story.

Come sit on my lap, and your Uncle Stockbroker will tell you all about the Great Stock Themes. These stories have helped promoters and brokers inflate notions into concepts and then into corporations. The ideas are timeless, even if the companies are not. Remember, a salesperson can't go wrong preempting the facts with a little truth:

1. **The Major New Product Drama**

2. **The New Form of Merchandising Story**

3. **The New Method of Production Tale**

4. **The Meaning of New Management Saga**

5. **The Cyclical Growth Legend***

6. **The Undervalued Asset Parable**

7. **The Big Event Fable**

*If you experience cyclical growth, please consult a reputable physician.

It only takes a short phone call to pitch a stock. But brokers who successfully sell a lot of shares almost always use a stock story to get their message across. This is so because each stock story automatically focuses their client's attention to the sexiest aspect of a given corporation.

In other words, a good broker saves his breath by telling an investor just what he wants to know. But nothing more. In this way he can end his sales call with a direct request for an order. And then repeat the process over and over again to new prospects.

Stock stories also allow hard-charging brokers to save time on research. As time passes, a corporation's new product may prove to be a dud. Its management incompetent. Its merchandising or manufacturing schemes ludicrous. Or its entire industry may go out of fashion.

Investors may be shaken up by these corporate developments, but a broker who works smart need not worry. He can keep selling the same company's shares simply by telling a different stock story. This is how veteran brokers build enormous client positions. Of course, if all of the above disasters happen to a broker's favorite company, stock stories #6 and #7 quickly come into play.

Any company that hapless is ripe for a hostile takeover. A storytelling broker need only recite how "The Undervalued Asset Parable" could lead to "The Big Event Fable" coming true to convince all of his clients to double up on their positions.

Should I do my own research?

To 99.9% of all registered representatives, original research means reading the newspaper or another firm's research reports. Any situation that fits one of the above seven great stock stories will sell no matter how you came across the company, so do yourself a favor and worry about research *after* you've sold as much of the stock as possible.

As a broker, what is my upside? Downside? Legal exposure?

If your stocks go up, the client equity you control will increase exponentially. Most clients will leave profits in their accounts to ride on the next trade. Even better, you will be immediately flooded with referrals. To your amazement the amount of equity you raise will increase as you decrease the time you devote to selling. More importantly, thanks to your first score, you'll be calling the shots on asset allocation and market timing—not the clients. You'll never photocopy an S & P sheet again!

The downside? See financial planning section in this chapter.

As to legal exposure, forget about it, so long as you stick to the truth and avoid the facts.

World headquarters of Denver Penny Stock Market. Membership: 25 cents.

What firms market this product?

Are you pulling our legs? Everyone sells stocks. Few can earn a living at it.

Okay. Since I'm gonna be a stockbroker, I might as well sell stocks. What are some buzzwords?

Forget about buzzwords. Stick to telling stories.

Futures

Futures speculators make money by outwitting the market, placing continuous bets that they know something now that markets will discover later.

Smart brokers never forget that futures are a zero sum game—half win and half lose. Thanks to generous commissions, brokers almost always end up on the better half of the deal.

Most well-informed clients know something about the futures markets. The explosive growth in futures contracts for financial instruments and the introduction of stock-index futures have tied the once remote futures markets to the most familiar investments.

You'll have to tell clients that while futures are in fact contracts to deliver a commodity at a specified date, profits are the only commodity that they'll ever have to take delivery on. Key to your sales pitch is the enormous leverage futures provide: relatively small amounts of money can

An early 1950s commodities transaction.

control industrial-strength quantities of the underlying commodity.

What's the commission?

From $50 to $150 per contract.

What does this mean for me?

A Jaguar 12-cylinder performance sedan and a closetful of Italian designer fashions. One client dollar in a futures account should earn a broker at least twenty cents in commissions over a year.

Whoa! Where am I going to find prospects willing to take the plunge?

You can start by selling to business people involved in markets with price risks that can be hedged by futures contracts. An owner of a large apartment building will buy heating oil futures. Farmers regularly reduce their risk with futures in agricultural commodities. Even Mafia loan sharks like to hedge their portfolios with interest-rate futures contracts.

You're not, however, limited to clients interested in futures for strictly business-related purposes. A potential speculator is anyone with the active or latent desire to reach for the golden ring (and probably end up losing far more than his initial investment). As long as your client has available cash in an account, you can start trading with impunity. Never start trading with only an IOU! The only good faith in the futures business is cleared funds. If a client has at least $5000 in cleared funds available in a trading account, he has definite potential as a futures speculator. Financial derelicts; underachievers; lazy, arrogant offspring of wealthy, hardworking families; masochists and suicidal manic depressives are the types you're looking for.

Is it a good prospecting tool?

Works like a lightning rod in a Montana thunder boomer. Everyone has an

emotional response to futures trading. Anyone who reads a newspaper or watches the evening news should have a dangerously half-formed opinion about OPEC, interest rates or the weather that can become the seed of a futures trade. The possibility of turning uninformed opinions into cold cash is irresistible to some. Even clients so withdrawn from reality so as not to have opinions can be impressed by a carefully constructed sales discourse on the trends in specific markets.

Sounds great. What's the bottom line?

Of the many different futures markets available, one will always be "hot." You will never run out of stories or commissionable products. You only need twenty halfway decent accounts to make a nice living from a futures business. Twenty

$25,000 trading accounts will generate more than $100,000 in gross commissions a year.

On the negative side, you'll need a strong stomach to be able to face clients after their equity has been destroyed in a flurry of margin calls. Handling futures accounts also exposes you dangerously to trading and execution errors. Because of the large number of transactions—many in the same day, some in the same minute—such errors are inevitable. You will end up eating all the errors, simply because no firm wants the publicity involved in defending a commodity broker. A final drawback is that you or somebody who sounds just like you must stay by your phone during trading hours.

I hear it's a dangerous, unregulated market.

Nonsense! The exchanges are self-regulating. Except

to a handful of crypto-commissars ensconced in bureaucratic ivory towers, the social machinery constructed by individuals engaged in the exchange and distribution of the earth's basic commodities is a beautiful sight to behold.

I love free enterprise but don't want to get sued. How vulnerable am I to wrathful clients?

If a prospect is absolutely ignorant about financial affairs, what jury wouldn't think that you hornswoggled him into blowing his life savings? Even more dangerous are the apparently innocent prospects who know how to take advantage of you and your firm by sticking you with errors and suits seeking punitive damages. Don't let these pitfalls worry you: the risk disclosure documents that a client must sign should protect you in just about any circumstance.

Aren't a lot of commodity and futures firms going bankrupt or scaling back their activities?

Disinflation has been a killer for the industry as a whole, but the potential for creative, aggressive individuals with large egos is unlimited. Remember, one dollar of client money in futures generates the same commission as ten dollars of the same money in stocks!

What else do I need to know?

As with all highly leveraged speculative pursuits, the common language is the jargon of technical analysis. Some brokers and traders actually go off the deep end with charting and trend analysis. Computers make it even worse, seducing many investors into believing that they've taken hold of coincidence and have discovered a new "economic law." Some victims of self-deception believe they have

During a lull in trading, these professional market scalpers enjoy a contemplative moment.

found a surefire trading "system" to be implemented in a "program."

The nice thing about speculative clients is that if they don't lose it all in their first trade they become self-proclaimed "experts." From then on, all you have to do is report price quotes and your clients will go crazy with trading orders.

Tell me a good way to get started in this racket.

One favorite approach is to play the market in "August" pork bellies, the commodity from which bacon is made. In that month, the price of pork bellies is believed to be influenced by the quality of the tomato crop. If tomatoes are juicy and delicious, more people are going to make bacon, lettuce and tomato sandwiches, thus increasing the consumption of bacon. Anticipation of a good tomato year will up the value of the pork belly contract as August nears. Playing August bellies is what is known as the "BLT" spread. A somewhat unscrupulous broker could advise half his clients to go "long" (bet on a price increase) and the other half to go "short" (bet on a price decrease). Half the clients will lose, but the broker never goes hungry.

BLT: The favorite lunchtime sandwich for hardworking commodities pros.

Insurance

"When they first told me I had to sell insurance, why, I put my head in a tin can and banged up on it real good," recalls Bob Deerhefer, an E. F. Hutton broker in Omaha.

Today, Bob derives almost one-fifth of his annual income from selling insurance—and he hasn't had a headache in years.

Stockbrokers who sell insurance focus on two products:

☐ Universal Life Insurance (not a wholly owned subsidiary of a Korean religious cult) offers high yields on cash accumulated in the contract and comparatively low premiums in relation to the level of the death benefits.

☐ Single-Premium Tax-Deferred Annuities (SPDAs) appeal to clients because they can accumulate interest without paying current taxes. Brokers market SPDAs along with tax-free municipal bonds as garden-variety tax shelters.

Brokers who sell these two products go after only the prime retail insurance customers. Because the products are relatively simple, the broker doesn't need to waste time with a complicated sales pitch or get wrapped up in the hassle of acting as an all-purpose insurance agent.

What's in it for your clients? That's easy. They can get low-cost insurance without having to sit through an insurance agent's extended kitchen-table spook session.

So what is the commission?

For Universal Life products, gross commissions range from 50 percent of first-year premiums to as much as 100 percent, and you'll get a small residual commission for the life of the policy.

When you sell SPDAs, the gross commission should be $50 per $1000 invested in the single premium.

Surprisingly, a broker's

payout comes to about half of what a full-line insurance agent could earn.

So how do I get started?

Don't give your clients the impression that you take insurance seriously—offer it as an incidental benefit, an offhand way to save a few dollars. They'll never suspect that insurance is the financial equivalent of rust-coating at an auto dealership—a high-markup product that's hard not to buy.

To get your insurance business rolling, find a company marketing a competitive product with an attractive commission structure. Then canvass your entire client and prospect book and hit them with your pitch.

Never accept any offers to become an "insurance coordinator" for your branch. It's okay to earn commissions from insurance products, but don't sully yourself in the details or paperwork that are the trademark of all insurance products.

Interest rates aren't everything. How about all those medical tests and actuarial tables?

Today's "new breed" insurer has a streamlined application procedure to accelerate approval. Medical examinations are obsolete as long as the broker answers all the questions on the application, writes legibly and never uses Wite-Out. Of course, some potential risks may be too heady for even the most aggressive underwriter. A heavy smoker, alcoholic, and heroin addict with a heart murmur might have to spill some urine in a "qualified" doctor's office before getting accepted. Ask your regional wholesaler or insurance coordinator for a list of "qualified" doctors.

Thanks! Anything else I have to do?

Pass your home state's life insurance examination and register with the insurance companies whose products you want to sell.

Managed Accounts

Can professional money managers do a better job than you can of investing your clients' money? No.

Can these pros at least do better than broad-based indices of financial markets? Absolutely not.

So why are we including "professionally" managed accounts in this Encyclopedia? That's simple: money managers sometimes do a good job, but no matter what, they're always profitable and fun to do business with.

Get to know a bunch of smart money runners as soon as you can. Put your clients' money under the control of the manager of your choice, sit back and watch the commissions roll in.

Then get ready to have some fun. Because a common outlook on things is the starting point in a successful "partnership," good times are definitely part of the agenda.

These typically include:

1. Racquetball at least once a week.
2. A mutual appreciation of this year's exquisite California vintages.
3. Dancing nude with Brazilian transvestites on the streets of Rio during *Carnaval*.
4. Flying sorties over Lebanon in unmarked Israeli warplanes.

Friendship and trust help eradicate the occupational cynicism that pervades the investment business and form the backbone of a successful relationship with your money managers.

Lay it on me. What's the commission?

As a quid pro quo for the assets you've raised, money managers will execute all trades involving clients' holdings through you. You can figure out the commission yields by reading everything else in this chapter. The manager's compensation is a percentage of the total assets under control, usually one-half of one percent to one percent.

So what is so great about having managed accounts?

Finding clients for money managers pays off immediately by exposing you to the most sophisticated and active investors in your community. Managed accounts generally have a $50,000 to $1 million minimum account size. Only wealthy individual investors or "institutional accounts" (i.e., pension funds, insurance companies or even small bank trust accounts) are qualified prospects.

Why not sell these folks on the benefits of mutual funds?

Yes, mutual funds and managed accounts have much in common: broad asset diversification, verifiable track records and liquidity. And yes, mutual funds are run by some of the same people that operate managed accounts.

But managed accounts deliver psychological benefits to your clients that can't be measured. Managers give the impression that each account is tailored to the investor's exact risk threshold and tax status. And we're talking Savile Row here. These rich folks like to be pampered!

When it comes time to close a sale you will find that a money manager is more than just a paper track record. Bring one to your town for a round of interviews and watch 'em sing and dance. A manager will close your sales for you. No mutual fund can do that.

Wow, what a deal! How do I get started?

Advisers with less than $100 million under management rarely get invited to appear in *Barron's* "Round Table Interviews," the leading public forum for money managers. That means that they depend on brokers to do their promotion and asset raising. Even so, finding a money manager with a strong investment record who will work with a retail broker is a difficult proposition. It actually requires more refined selling skills than finding qualified investors.

Your firm can help you by offering a number of "products" to dangle under the nose of a likely adviser: access to underwritings (preferably those above room temperature), active over-the-counter market making in target stocks, research, data banks or actually subletting data-processing facilities. These "products" are bartered for the adviser's transaction business. However, all of these incentives have little to do with the essential nature of corralling an adviser. It is the personal rapport or marketing chemistry that develops between you. There is no room for cynical posturing; true belief is required of both parties.

It sounds like something my mother would approve of. What can go wrong?

Any broker who discards the membrane of skepticism that protects him from the savage realities of this godless world invites eventual and total destruction. Job was lucky—he never played the market. Money managers get as soft as the commissions they dole out. Times change and will inevitably derail the most fortunate adviser and his broker dependents. Like any other market phenomenon, investment success eventually contradicts itself.

Well, at least I can't go to jail.

Maybe so, but if you have the misfortune to successfully promote some swindler professing financial genius—watch out. The wealthy, powerful pillars of your community that you inadvertently helped to rip off may seek revenge by endorsing your financial destruction and personal ruin. The high and mighty hate to be paraded before the hoi polloi as dupes.

Physical Metals

Hoarding a metal that may someday be in short supply is the essence of the Physical Metals game. Reps can offer the storage vaults of their firm as a service to physical metal buyers or ship it out to the customer. Shipping and storage are paid for by the client, as is any local sales tax due upon delivery and included in the COD billing to the client. In an era of disinflation, selling physical metals is a routine service operation, but at least it pays the broker.

What is the commission?

The same as agency stock business, about two percent.

Can I make a living at it?

The potential to make a good living by focusing exclusively on marketing metals to retail clients died with the great inflation-hedge bust of the early 1980s. This does not mean that physical metals should be shunned by alert brokers. The commissions are good, and at most firms a small but professional trading desk survives to process orders and back up the sales force.

THE CURB MARKET

From the day the first brokers met under a buttonwood tree in 1792 until the year the Curb Market moved indoors in 1921, New York finance always featured an outside securities market.

The most famous of all outside markets was the Curb. Its trading activities were located, for the most part, in the middle of Broad Street a half a block south of Wall. Of course the exchange wandered a bit during its formative years after the Civil War.

Curbstone brokers were not a part of New York's high society. They were seldom seen in the society pages of the *Times* and they didn't live on Fifth Avenue. Instead they commuted to the financial district from middle-class bungalows in Brooklyn, the Bronx or New Jersey.

Outdoor brokers were a

hardy lot who traded securities every business day of the year—rain, snow or shine. To communicate to their colleagues, who hung out of office windows above the street, Curb brokers perfected a series of hand signals and signs, creating what amounted to a new financial language.

Brokers conducted all aspects of securities trading in the street, stock transfers included. Any security that could be delivered could trade on the Curb.

Speculative new issues played an important part on the exchange. Often a young broker would rent a sandwich board announcing that he would be making a market in the new shares.

But the Curb was never just a sleazy penny stock market. Many of the world's strongest businesses chose to be listed on the Curb. Usually these

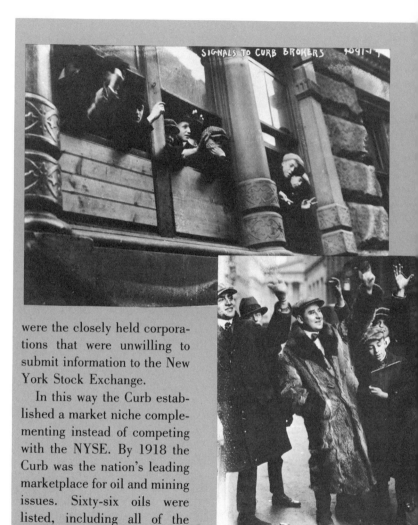

were the closely held corporations that were unwilling to submit information to the New York Stock Exchange.

In this way the Curb established a market niche complementing instead of competing with the NYSE. By 1918 the Curb was the nation's leading marketplace for oil and mining issues. Sixty-six oils were listed, including all of the Rockefeller Standard companies. Along with the oils, the Curb Market boasted seventy listed mining companies and eight industrials. Of course many of the listed shares were inactive. If trading occurred in fifty different issues it was considered to be a broad market on the Curb.

Some of the leading companies listed on the Curb in 1918 included: BAT, Gillette, Holly Sugar, S. S. Kresge, MacAndrews & Forbes, R. J. Reynolds Tobacco, Todd Ship Yards, Anglo-American Oil, Hecla Mining and, of course, all of the Standard companies.

The market-making strength of the exchange was challenged in 1911 during the great Standard Oil divestiture. Carl Pforzhemeimer, the leading specialist in Standard shares, led a group of brokers from the Curb's millionaires' row in a concerted effort to trade all of the new companies on a when-issued basis. His group had plenty of capital because many of the new Standard companies were trading at prices in excess of $1000 a share.

Middle-age prosperity or, perhaps, the influenza epidemic, convinced Curb brokers to vote for a move indoors. That was in 1921. Today the only outside market near Wall Street trades exclusively illegal commodities.

These pictures were taken by George G. Bain, an obscure and eccentric New York photographer. His photos, taken between 1908 and 1918, are the most comprehensive record of business life on the Curb.

What are physical metals?

The traditionally popular physical metals are gold, silver, and platinum molded into uniform bullion blocks or coins. The nonnumismatic coins are minted by governments and include gold Krugerrands from South Africa and the U.S. gold Maple Leaf. Bags of U.S. silver coins minted before 1964 are also popular.

Whom do I sell physical metals to?

Surveys at major firms show that about one quarter of the clients with stock accounts have bought or own coins or bullion. Physical metal buyers are not commodity traders. In fact, their buying psychology of "dollar averaging" has more in common with mutual-fund buyers than the Hunt brothers.

The most canny commodity broker in recent history was the guy who convinced the Hunt brothers to gamble away a fortune in metals. The broker sat at the brothers' kitchen table and held up a silver fork, asking, How much more will this cost next year? And the year after? Nelson Bunker Hunt became so enthusiastic over this homegrown observation about inflation that he spit out a mouthful of succotash and decided to corner the silver market.

But instead of hoarding physical metals he got greedy and tried to rig the silver futures market. Bunker and his brother lost hundreds of millions of dollars on their gamble.

Had they simply accumulated all of the silver coins, candelabras and butter knives in North America they would be richer men today.

As a broker, what is my upside? Downside? Legal exposure?

The upside is extra dollars in your pocket earned for assisting your clients in their effort to hedge against the long-term effects of inflation. Metals are in such bad repute among the general investing public that a hard sell is impossible. So make the most of it with a simple and pleasant offer to existing clients and prospects. Let them know that you can help them buy coins or bullion any time at their convenience.

The downside might occur if a salesperson actually becomes convinced that nuclear winter is inevitable, that condos in Nebraska salt mines are a steal, and that small arms ammo is a better buy than gold coins.

Legal exposure? As long as the business is a cash and deliver transaction, what can go wrong?

Money-Market Funds (Cash Management)

Money-market accounts are on the cutting edge of the changing financial services industry. That's why they're such a bloody mess.

If your firm didn't offer these accounts, the money in them would move to a bank or some other financial institution. These competitors don't have to pay commissions to salesmen—and in the case of money-market accounts, neither does your firm. Retail brokers earn no commissions for selling them. So why should you sell them? Why do lemmings run off cliffs?

With the addition of check writing and credit/debit card access, the basic money-market account has evolved into the more elaborate Cash Management Account (CMA). Merrill Lynch first developed CMAs in the late 1970s, and today any brokerage firm wishing to do business with the general public must offer some variant of it.

Apart from the inexorable jackboot of history, what's behind the CMA? Just a bunch of T-bills and other uninteresting short-term money-market securities a broker needn't worry about until the Coming Financial Apocalypse blows down the whole stinking house of cards!

No commissions. You can't be serious.

Retail brokers net nothing by selling money-market funds, and very little for moving short-term instruments like T-bills and certificates of deposit (CDs).

But almost every broker sells these instruments as a service to their clients.

Service, without commissions? Sounds like a fancy word for slavery.

Selling money-market investments may be a form of white-collar cotton picking, but the broker is actually benefiting for one key reason: the client's money stays under his control. Short-term securities are often "book entry." This means that there is no certificate to ship to the client and the cash stays in the account under the watchful eye of the full-service broker. This can be a lifesaver during prolonged bear markets, when a broker's only sustaining hope is the client equity parked in money-market instruments awaiting the day when the "buy low" sales pitch becomes effective.

Accounts that combine check writing, a credit/debit card and a money-market fund in a standard security account work like flypaper on unsuspecting new customers because of the complicated credit agreements that a client must sign to open the account. Once they're in, it's virtually impossible to get out. This is good until you decide to move to another firm.

So you only sell this stuff to keep your clients under your thumb?

Yes. But selling these dull things does more than simply retain client equity: it is sometimes a form of low-cost psychotherapy for war-weary producers. Many disabled or burned-out commodity and option brokers trying to readjust to office life after electroshock treatments will spend hours on end selling T-bills and money-market funds. Branch office managers know that when the electrons finally stop bouncing around in the craniums of these brokers, the retained client equity will provide excellent fodder for the options and futures markets.

Mutual Funds

Imagine a product that's virtually the same as another product—except it costs more because a sales force has to be paid.

Now stop imagining and start selling, because what we're talking about is front-end load mutual funds.

In their infinite wisdom, front-end funds pay brokers handsome commissions for finding new investors (unlike the so-called "no-load" funds that are of no interest here).

At one time many brokers sneered at the idea of selling mutual funds. Then Congress came up with a brilliant idea called the Individual Retirement Account (IRA). IRAs allow people to put money into tax-deferred retirement plans each year. What better way to prepare for the collapse of the Social Security system?

Mutual funds make ideal IRA investments because each share in the mutual-fund investment company represents an interest in the fund's diversified assets. Brokers cannot take IRA mutual investments too lightly, because the competition will grab this client money with no problem.

Remember, mutual funds are *sold*, not *bought*. Failure to sell them will result in Mutual (Fund) Assured Destruction (MAD).

What's the commission?

Mutual funds are the granddaddy of all high-commission financial-package products. Commissions range from six percent to ten percent of the dollars invested.

So whom do I sell mutual funds to?

Every potential client has or will have an IRA. Demand this business out of mutual respect.

As a broker, what is my upside? Downside? Legal exposure?

Your upside is earning commissions by selling front-end load mutual funds.

The downside is an excruciatingly boring career.

Legal exposure? Without commissions, who can afford legal problems?

New Issues

In the brokerage lexicon, references to various parts of the human anatomy are common. One favorite is the "hot button," or that part of the client's physiognomy that activates buying. If your timing is right, there's no better way to hit a client's hot button than with a just-issued share of a hot new stock.

Selling new issues to the public brings in lots of money to brokerage firms that underwrite them. However, huge outlays for such overhead expenses as legal fees, financial printing, Beefeater martinis, red suspenders, and daily shoeshines tend to add to the up-front risk.

New issues find their way to the market through a friendly grouping of brokerage firms known ominously as "syndicates," headed up by a lead underwriter. Firms always invite each other to join one another's selling groups so as not to be excluded in any future underwriting. This tea-party atmosphere is celebrated the next day when a broker/dealer guest list is published as part of a "tombstone" advertisement.

Brokers involved with any underwriting always ask each other, "Will it work?" If a deal "works," the sales force doesn't have to.

What are the commissions on a new issue?

Plenty! Your firm can earn concessions of up to 10 percent of the amount raised in an underwriting. You share in this largesse according to the payout of your firm. Always check for the pertinent details in the prospectus offering the issue.

So whom do I sell new issues to?

During the periodic fire storms of speculative activity, investors scramble madly to put their money into initial public offerings (IPOs). The frenzy feeds on itself as investors become obsessed with placing orders only for underwritings expected to be "oversubscribed" (when orders exceed the total number of available shares). The shrewdest, greediest investors have a complete knowledge of the allocation procedures used by underwriters and brokers and will attempt to curry your favor in hope of getting a piece of the action. Their number-one investment criterion for any offering boils down to a single question mumbled in shorthand centigrade: "How hot is it?"

Do you mean new issues can sell themselves?

You don't have to be Sylvia Porter to figure that out. The sad part is that every time a "sure thing" comes around the average retail broker's share allocation is nil. To avoid getting snubbed, either bypass new issues entirely or make sure to participate in all of your firm's underwritings to get a nice cut of each deal.

Sounds great. Put me on the short list—I'm going long new issues!

One thing that might be long is that rope around your neck! New issues can be dangerous. Clients are not obligated by an order for a new issue until they have read a final prospectus. Underwriters don't print the final prospectus until after they've sold the deal. Some clients use this right as an excuse to regurgitate their purchases if an issue fails to appreciate instantly, leaving the broker (and his pet) to eat the losses.

How can brokers afford the risk of doing new-issue business?

First, don't sell a new issue to a client you don't know, trust or having something on. Second, cultivate a friendly relationship with some hedge funds.

Hedge funds?

Hedge funds are investment pools that buy new issues at the initial offering price and then resell them when secondary trading begins, sometimes making a large profit along the way. Hedge funds have an uncanny predisposition to reverse telephone charges when calling a broker. Hedge funds add to their mystery by frequently mak-ing purchases through shell corporations or under assumed names. In the great tradition of all traders, only first names like Sol, Ivan, Larry, or Bruce are used by hedge fund operatives.

Firms unanimously condemn hedge funds and will go to extreme lengths to protect their underwritings from being clipped by the hedgies. This is impossible due to the archaic distribution policies of all syndicate departments and the shrewd maneuvering of the fund operatives.

What firms market new issues?

When times are good, your grandmother could hang out a shingle and pump out new issues.

Options

Some people think of options as a hopelessly confusing abstract concept. Others say they are a highly leveraged, limited-downside investment strategy. Still others call them an invitation to self-destruction. But for a broker, options are quite simply one of the most commission-rich products around.

Options represent a way for speculators to profit from changes in the price of an underlying asset, and from the hopes, dreams and fears of other speculators. Specifically, they are contracts giving the right to sell (a put) or to buy (a call)

GO FOR IT, AMERICA!

Americans are happier with their investments today than they were ten years ago! That's the surprising and encouraging result of an exhaustive nationwide survey conducted recently by a top securities-industry research group.

The startling fact is this: A mind-boggling 80 percent of America's investors are happy with their current portfolios.

But what is the real story behind the statistics? Most of the respondents to the confidential twenty-page questionnaire admitted to previous investment fiascoes. But their confidence remains undaunted and their good feelings nearly unanimous—despite predictions of gloom and doom about the economy foisted on the public by the naysaying media prognosticators.

How do people ignore the headlines and expert warnings about deficits, recession and inflation? Can they really sleep well at night on mattresses stuffed full of brokerage house statements and confirmations?

Of course they can. Here's how:

PATIENCE

"I kept hoping that the market would get better. Without my broker calling me every other day for more money—I think I would have given up."

Almost half of the investors—42 percent—didn't join the stampede of media panic. They waited out financial turbulence—and it did get better.

LAUGHTER

"It looked like I had blown $50,000 on a river barge leasing tax shelter. I wanted to cry.

"But my broker laughed and pointed out that I could immediately write off the whole investment. Then he showed me how I could increase my upside by organizing a class action suit against his firm.

"Now I'm laughing too."

Fifty-five percent of those surveyed consider a sense of humor very important to successful investing. Although a minority 12 percent thought their brokers were laughing at them instead of with them.

THE IRA REVOLUTION

"I'm twenty-six years old, and I have a good career in marketing. I hope to marry and have children when my fiancée gets out of the Marines. She has electronics training and should have no problem finding a job.

"But the most important thing in my life is that I will be an IRA multimillionaire by the end of the century."

A simple desire to be rich is the most important consideration of investors of all ages. The IRA has instilled new hope and optimism about affluence in respondents under forty.

FINANCIAL PLANNING

"I wanted to go for broke. But my financial consultant taught me the importance of diversification. She helped me reduce my overall risk—without altering my long-term goals.

"One big hit is all I need to pay for mediocre returns on the rest of my portfolio. That is why I now own positions in three different gourmet ice cream franchises and two custom-design chocolate chip cookie firms.

"Sure I know that one or two of them will go belly up—but gourmet 'grazing' is the fastest-growing industry in the country. And the one company that survives the competition will become the GM of the service economy by 1990."

Eighty percent of those surveyed feel that investment professionals are better trained, more informed, and better equipped to handle their accounts than ever before.

TOGETHERNESS

"When the market is down, I stay with my broker for tax reasons. But when the market is up he is the best friend an investor like me could ever have."

Commitment and hope are the glue that keep a broker/client relationship together during lean years. Fifty-six percent said that they personally liked their broker very much.

From this sampling nearly half hoped that their broker might someday find a steadier line of work because of deep concern about their RR's health.

Undeniably, the common thread running through all of the respondents' answers and personal testimony is that the financial services industry has done a spectacular job.

Even more important, individual stockbrokers have achieved an unprecedented degree of success in determining and fulfilling their clients' investment needs.

People care. About themselves, their money and their stockbrokers. Family values are making a comeback. In marriage. In child rearing. And, most dramatically, in the emotional bond between brokers and their clients.

Financial security is the bedrock of investor confidence today. And the full-service broker is the number-one guardian of this most important American value.

at a specific price at a specified time in the future.

In the old days, stocks were the only financial substance that could legally and efficiently be optioned. Sellers literally had to "write" a contract of sale before searching out a buyer and negotiating a price. Brokers who handled these over-the-counter option transactions were often denigrated by more respectable members of the financial community, never receiving invitations to Christmas parties at the exchange.

Then along came some bright young folk from the Chicago Board Options Exchange who put opportunity and modern data processing together to invent the world's first listed options market. Eager to create new trading vehicles, the boys from LaSalle Street rationalized the transfer of puts and calls by standardizing contracts and processing all settlements through a single clearing house, as in the futures exchanges.

Listed options have flourished. Commodities, debt, stock indices and currencies have all now joined individual stock as options vehicles. Regional stock exchanges benefit tremendously from their market-making activities in various option contracts.

Believe it or not, there are still quite a few firms on the street that don't have the data-processing capacity to provide the support an options broker needs. At such firms the primitiveness of the computers is matched by the dimness of the managing executives. Financial evolution will not be kind to these firms: in a few years some department store chain will buy them and impose minimum production quotas in options on the entire sales force.

What's the commission?

Approximately two percent to five percent of the purchase price, based on a sliding scale combining the number of contracts and the dollar value of the contracts.

Say that one more time—slowly. Even better, show me a commission schedule so I can figure out what you mean.

No can do. Rates change so often at major firms that no one ever has an up-to-date copy available.

Okay. When was the last time retail commission rates were lowered?

No comment.

So tell me, what will one dollar of client equity earn in commissions a year?

From 12 cents to 100 cents on the dollar, depending on how long your client's luck holds out.

Wow! **Who buys these things?**

First, never forget that you're not actually selling options. What you're selling is an "option strategy." These strategies are sold to numbers junkies, the kind of people who as adults can still do arithmetic sums in their heads without the aid of a pocket calculator. Studies show that a majority of options speculators are engineers, computer programmers, accountants, professors, small-business proprietors and serial murderers. Options speculators tend to have postgraduate degrees (further evidence of the enormous value of higher education) and tend to live outside of the Northeast corridor.

Options speculators, like their brethren in the futures pits, use personal computers and experiment with investment software. Options clients are smart and they pack some heavy-duty firepower with them when they want to blow their money to bits.

These hackers may be geniuses, but I'm too dumb to figure out what the heck you're talking about. Help!

Options trading holds such strong appeal to people fascinated with numbers, ratios and other value relationships because of the range of options contracts trading in a single category. For a given future month, a stock currently trading at 50 might have a schedule of options contracts pricing the same security at 40, 45, 50, 55 and 60. This range of so-called "strike prices" invites a speculator to buy and sell contracts in various combinations, "spreads" and "straddles" in an attempt to maximize leverage while going after a big profit dependent on a specific outcome. Clients become deeply wrapped up in this complicated speculation as their fascination with the price relationship between different options months and strike prices instensifies. This is where the big commissions come in, since the number of transactions involved in setting up a strategy, modifying it in midstream and then winding it down is so great. The broker is the only party exercising an option with a 100 percent chance of profit!

Is it a good prospecting tool?

Indeed, options are the most seductive of all investment vehicles. But to sell options you must have the capacity to speak authoritatively about an ever-changing array of mind-bogglingly complicated options strategies.

Tax Shelters

Tax-shelter promoters have an old saying: You've got to lose money to make money. This philosophy makes tax shelters perfect for the retail investor.

How do tax shelters arrange for clients to lose money? The deals include such exciting endeavors as energy exploration, equipment leasing, show biz production, high-tech research and development, animal husbandry and real estate. Each deal is structured as a limited partnership, with the losses and other tax benefits flowing directly to your clients.

The general partners (GPs) who run and promote tax shelters flourish beyond even a politician's dream of avarice. This is good because most GPs will pay a broker very handsomely for finding willing investors.

What's the commission?

Eighty to one hundred dollars on each $1000 invested, with $5000 the smallest investment unit.

That sounds pretty damn good, but once I direct client money into a limited partnership that equity will never earn me another commission, will it?

True, limited partnerships are illiquid. But hefty up-front commissions are often just the first installment of what you'll net on a deal. When your firm packages its own tax shelters—usually in partnership with an outside shelter promoter—you can expect hefty "back-end participation." This gives a broker a piece of the profits realized when the underlying asset involved in the shelter is either refinanced or resold through the brokers who originally marketed the deal. It may take six to ten years for a deal to "flip"—a virtual eternity in the time horizon of an aggressive broker. A fringe benefit of tax-shelter marketing takes the form of gifts from the sponsor ranging from fountain pens to all-expenses-paid weekends in Vegas.

I like it, but whom do I sell tax shelters to?

Anybody with a social security number, cash or access to a line of credit. The minimum net worth requirement for a publicly registered partnership is "20/20," $20,000 in assets (outside of home furnishings) and $20,000 in income. Such deals are strictly low-rent, though. The truly rich account for an enormous chunk of tax-shelter business: many private placements have $50,000 to $150,000 minimums. One of these a month and you've got it made. In refining your

A member of the Future Stockbrokers of America shows off his first homemade tax shelter.

sales pitch, don't forget that investing in tax shelters is a necessary requirement for the self-image of the very wealthy. When was the last time you heard someone boast about how much he paid in taxes last year? Earning big money and avoiding taxes go hand in hand.

Is it a good prospecting tool?

Shelters are simple to sell because you only have to learn one generic sales pitch that you can use for any shelter you'll ever have to sell. Keep your pitch simple, and eager clients will plunk down $50,000 as if they were buying a Swiss-cheese sandwich at the corner deli. This can become almost intoxicating, particularly when you see how one sale pays you for the time it takes to pitch fifty prospects.

Soon you'll come to love the ease with which you can

sell these wondrous tax-avoidance schemes. Accountants and lawyers wired into the deal will send you an endless procession of referrals. All you have to do is sell: your firm and the product sponsor make it as easy as possible for you by providing all the backup you need, including handling the nitty-gritty of closings.

What is my upside? Downside? Legal exposure?

The upside is complex. Unlike most other investments, tax shelters make clients ecstatic about the losses that pile up year after year. The more money the client loses, the more he throws into tax-advantaged deals, and the more business you get as close friends of the client rush to get into the action. Once somebody gets hooked on deferring taxes (all shelters really do is defer judgment day), maturing deals force them into even heavier reliance on shelters to defer the tax bite. Shelter buyers turn into junkies, and you're the candy man. Not bad for a guy or gal who gets the title of "tax-shelter specialist."

The downside is simple: most deals packaged for sale to the public have to roll off an assembly line that ignores underlying economic realities. The commissions, fees and asset "puffing" that make shelters so profitable to promoters and salesmen make most deals truly dubious to investors. Even if you put a client into a sincerely well-conceived shelter, the client's shelter can sour if subsequent deals put out by the same sponsor fall apart. This happens all too frequently: after all, general partners and shelter promoters live well and could hardly afford to stop putting deals together simply because of changes in their fundamental businesses. At their worst, all tax-shelter promotions are bubbles that take years to pop, and then an eternity for client reimbursement. Fortunately, deals go sour years after you sell them, well beyond a client's memory and thus his capability for holding a grudge.

Legal exposure? None. There are more lawyers at a firm's tax-shelter department than in the local hospital after a major airplane disaster. Let them worry—you are just a simple peddler.

What about changes in the tax laws?

Possible changes in the tax laws actually add to the allure of shelters. Authoritative talk about the IRS and Congress never fails to impress a prospect. Don't forget to memorize this standard speech: "Don't worry, this deal has been *immunized* and your pay-in will be reduced by the legislative decline in marginal tax rates. Anyway, this deal is sure to be grandfathered under the old law; it may be your last chance to maximize your opportunity before tax rates change." Opera stars have to study for years and consume more than 25 tons of linguine be-

fore they can sing a song this sweet!

Venture Capital

Contrary to popular myth, not all venture capitalists live in Silicon Valley, drive Saab Turbos, or peruse business plans while lolling in hot tubs. Even in regions of the country where lolling is prohibited, venture capitalists thrive.

A broker can get into venture-capital deals by introducing likely entrepreneurs to established venture backers. You never know which of your clients will come up with a great business idea, but it happens—especially when their life savings start to evaporate due to market losses.

What's in it for me?

Your compensation is an equity stake in a small growth company. Your equity usually takes the form of warrants. Warrants, which are similar to options, give holders the right to buy shares at a specified price sometime in the future.

As the middleman between entrepreneur and venture capitalist you should receive a portion of these warrants. This means you become a long-term investor in some risky venture—edible microchips or kosher pig farming, for example.

The cost of financing a good idea should not bankrupt a fledgling concern or water down the entrepreneur's stake in the venture. Unless you are operating with a lawyer or a fraud, venture-capital placement should not generate up-front commissions or fees.

What does all that mean in dollars and cents?

If the company shines you will have created an equity stake for yourself and potential finder's fees associated with any future financings, like going public (see new issues for further details).

I have a hard enough time finding a good plumber. Where do I find these venture folks?

Almost every region of the country has investors known for financing start-ups. Seek out venture capitalists who have been in business for a decade or two, and get to know the key people and the kind of opportunities that they understand. A skilled venture capitalist is a shrewd judge of character, and a customer's man must have a lot on the ball to make a good impression. But don't be shy. Venture capitalists need a vast web of correspondents in the hinterlands to filter good opportunities their way.

As a broker, what is my upside? Downside? Legal exposure?

If you ask me that one more time, I'm going to hit you upside your downside—and I don't care what my legal exposure is!

CHAPTER · 4

THE ONE-MINUTE BIG PICTURE

If you're like most brokers, an "investment philosophy" is something you need for your sales pitch—if one philosophy doesn't work, you look for one that does. "Information" is what you use to get people to stop thinking.

However, there may come a time when this pragmatic approach to the market becomes unsatisfying. At that moment, you will confront the obvious: lots of people are making big money by speculating and investing in the market. And you aren't one of them.

How do these people do it? Are they smart? Are they better informed? Are they just lucky? Or do they have some systematic approach to investing that can be successfully duplicated?

Artificial Dissemination

To find out how other people make millions in the market, you may want to undertake a serious study of economics and finance. It's only then that you will reassess your most important information resource. Your trash receptacle.

There you will find piles of research and information that your firm has spent millions to provide. Instead of scouring this stuff for new ways to sell products to clients, you're now looking for investments to buy for yourself. The average pile of discarded material will include:

1. Reports on industries and specific companies written by "analysts."

2. Overall economic forecasting.

"Who's smarter: Henry Kaufman or Joe Granville?"

"Is this economic recovery a stud or a dud?"

3. Charts showing the daily volume and price changes of stocks and other securities prepared by a "technical analyst."

4. A variety of business publications, ranging from the familiar, large-circulation slick magazines to obscure trade journals and newsletters.

5. Documents from publicly held companies, including annual reports and filings with the SEC.

6. Government statistics, including crucial CIA moisture reports covering wheat-growing areas of the Soviet Union.

Trying to make sense of all this data can bust your brain. It took an army of Nobel Prize–winning economists, computer experts and out-of-work rainmakers to put it down on paper. By the time you're done reading, you may be smart, but you'll also be poor—you just wasted an entire day.

The folks who keep your in-box full and trash can brimming mesh together as gears in a contraption peculiar to free-market societies. Like you, they are cogs in an awesome information dissemination machine. We call this apparatus The Perpetual Motion Prognostication Machine (PMPM).

ON TIME PERFORMANCE

The popular press rarely rivets the public's gaze on Wall Street. Many prognosticators have attempted to measure the effect of *Time* magazine covers on the stock market. Some experts see a stock market cover story as a sell signal. Others as a buy. Indeed, like any other reliable stock market indicator, the cover of *Time* will predict market trends 50 percent of the time.

No one knows how much money Time Inc.'s founder, Henry Luce, may have made on good stock market tips. But the editors at *Time* have deemed the market worthy of cover treatment seven times since the magazine's first issue:

YOUNG WALL STREET BULL	—June 14, 1948
WALL STREET BULL	—June 5, 1950
THE BULL MARKET	—January 10, 1955
WALL STREET BULL	—March 24, 1958
WALL STREET BULL	—December 29, 1958
BEAR VS. BULL ON WALL STREET	—June 1, 1962
BULL MARKET—OLÉ	—September 1, 1982

The savvy investor can choose from a wide variety of powerful investment philosophies.

Wall Street leaders have also gotten plenty of exposure on the cover of *Time*. How many of the following names ring a bell for you?

A. Cutten, Arthur W.
B. Estes, Billie Sol
C. Funston, Keith
D. Housser, Harry B.
E. Kahn, Otto H.
F. McCarthy, Michael W.

G. Martin, William McChesney, Jr.
H. Pickens, T. Boone
I. Robinson, Dwight P.
J. Stein, Howard
K. Thomson, James E.
L. Whitney, Richard

ANSWERS

A. Chicago stockbroker—December 10, 1928.
B. Tax-shelter promoter—May 25, 1962.
C. New York Stock Exchange President—Nov. 21, 1955.
D. Legitimate businessman—April 5, 1937.
E. Opera lover and Kuhn Loeb executive—November 2, 1925.
F. Merrill Lynch Chairman—May 31, 1963.
G. New York Stock Exchange President—August 15, 1938, and Federal Reserve Board Chairman—September 10, 1956.
H. Corporate raider—March 4, 1985.
I. Trustee Massachusetts Investors Growth Funds—June 1, 1959.
J. Dreyfus Mutual Fund President and Chief Executive—August 24, 1970.
K. Merrill Lynch President and Operations Head—August 19, 1966.
L. New York Stock Exchange President—February 26, 1934.

"Where's the market headed?"

THE SMART-CLIENT PROBLEM

It is astonishing what foolish things one can temporarily believe if one thinks too long alone.
—*J. M. Keynes*

What happens when an RR comes across a potential client who is rich, smart and not likely to be impressed with an off-the-shelf investment philosophy? It's what we call the Smart-Client Problem (SCP).

John Maynard Keynes, the famous economist, was a smart client (SC). RRs interested in learning how to handle SCs should study how his stockbrokers serviced his peculiar speculative appetites, a case study in how to solve the SCP.

Whether speculating in currencies for a private investment partnership or attending to the portfolio of Cambridge University, Keynes always required the services of hard-nosed customer's men.

Throughout the City of London Keynes was known as a plunger. He would daringly use borrowed money to maximize the leverage on his investments, causing his liquid net worth to fluctuate wildly.

Keynes required the services of two customer's men: O. T. Falk and Ian Macpherson. Falk, an acquaintance of Keynes's from the wartime Treasury office was a partner at Buckmaster & Moore. He promoted Keynes's skill as an economist and investor. The two founded three private partnerships and joined the boards of two insurance companies to direct their investments. Falk was an elegant hustler.

But it was the steady, service-oriented Macpherson who eventually won most of Keynes's commission business.

Macpherson proved to be unshakable no matter how extravagant Keynes's speculations. One Monday morning his clerk informed him of a classic SCP: Keynes had cornered the market on wheat. Said the clerk to his stunned boss: "I was playing golf in Sandwich at the weekend and saw all those ships going around to enter the Thames.

Did you not know [Keynes] in one form or another has acquired about one month's supply of wheat for the whole of this country?"

Smart clients often do this sort of thing to their brokers. But adventure and the commissions usually make any fiasco worth overcoming.

When Keynes confidently sauntered into Macpherson's office, the broker patiently listened to his brilliant client's scheme to defer accepting delivery of the wheat contracts he owned—his strategy was to demand that all the wheat be tested for "infestations" before he would take it. Keynes further explained that he had a fallback plan: he had measured a campus chapel and found it to be big enough to hold much of the commodity.

Keynes's squeeze on spot wheat had started out as an innocent straddle between Chicago and Buenos Aires prices. A month later, Keynes finally closed out his trade. No food riots had occurred and he had broken even before commissions.

Everything You Know Is Already Somebody Else's Idea

Even if you had a bigger trash can, the extra cubic inches of information wouldn't help you beat the market. Face it—somebody dumped this stuff on you, in just the same way you dump it on your clients. The PMPM works so well that the information it disseminates usually isn't worth very much. It's virtually impossible to know something everybody else doesn't know too.

Ask somebody smart, perhaps the first person you meet who has a calculator strapped to his belt, and you'll learn that significant information about a security instantly enters into the decisions and expectations of all market participants. This is what's known as the Efficient Market Theory (thank God it's only a theory—if markets are so efficient, how come brokers make so much money?).

If you stumble into the same smart fellow again, he'll no doubt want to keep talking about financial-market theories. Fortunately, you only have to know one more. It's called the Random Walk, and it's still going strong after three decades. Random Walkers contend that the price of a security is exactly what it should be. You pay for what you get. All known facts and expectations are incorporated into a market price. Only inherently unpredictable factors can change a price.

Prognostication is guesswork. Predicting the unpredictable is busywork. But

Louis XIV of Rukeyser: After disinflation, the only silver bubble left is his hairdo.

the PMPM keeps humming. Why? Future events haven't happened yet, and everybody wants in.

Polaroid Reality

Where does this leave you?

1. Your goal is to find clients and to make money by investing their money.
2. Your best and smartest clients want to feel "informed."
3. You must become a cog in the Perpetual Motion Prognostication Machine.
4. But it's all a Random Walk anyway.
5. Just like everyone else,

you're awash in an unpredictable reality.

In short, there is no Big Picture, except for Cecil B. De Mille reruns on TV. So when *The Ten Commandments* is on the late show, take the opportunity to prove this yourself. Hold a magnifying glass up to your television and you'll see that the picture is actually just a bunch of little dots. And in the financial services Big Picture, you're one of those dots.

This isn't to say, "You ain't nothing but a dot, so give up."

Far from it. We're telling you that your fate is not a Random Walk. Your lifetime game plan—to make a lot of money—doesn't have anything to do with predicting the future. It has to do with controlling it.

Predicting the future takes luck.

Manipulating the future takes skill.

INFORMATION IS NOT POWER. POWER IS POWER.

THE MX DART:
THROWING MONEY
AT THE PROBLEM

Money managers have always groused at the suggestion that a chimpanzee throwing a dart at the stock page can outperform a portfolio run by a $200,000-a-year MBA.

The sardonic editors at *Forbes* have rubbed it in by running a randomly selected "Dart Fund" of their own. And, lo and behold, the fund has outperformed most professionally managed funds tracked by the magazine.

Much to their credit, many enlightened money managers have acknowledged that the dart is in fact the best way to pick stocks. The result: the investment of millions in dart technology.

Financial services companies have spared no expense in their search for a better

dart, a dart that can achieve far better results than the familiar conventional dart.

Defense contractors have scrambled for Wall Street business. At the 1985 Paris Air Show, TRW unveiled the Smart Dart, a devastating laser-guided projectile that outperformed the S & P 500 by 12 percent during the first quarter of 1985. General Dynamics quickly countered with the sweep-wing MX Dart, a stock picker with pinpoint accuracy in preemptive market timing. And finally there is Mortek Corp.'s Stealth Dart, an undetectable stock picker that penetrates exchange airspace without detection by enemy floor traders and portfolio managers.

Wall Street's new-found en-

thusiasm for dartism has brought riches to the professional dart throwers of the United Kingdom, who have been aggressively recruited by the investment research departments of the major brokerage companies.

What's next in the booming dart industry? Most industry speculation now centers around the possibility of creating a defensive dart. Although it's still only in the theoretical stage, scientists believe that the technology exists to make a dart that could intercept other darts before they hit their targets. This could be of particular use to corporations intent on avoiding hostile takeover attempts.

CHAPTER 5

CASHING OUT: OH, TO BE NUDE IN CANCÚN!

Item. January, 1981: Donald Regan takes office as Secretary of the Treasury. His appointment to the key cabinet post tops a thirty-four-year career in financial services at Merrill Lynch, the nation's largest brokerage company. It was Regan who led the "Thundering Herd" to unprecedented prosperity and power.
Estimated net worth at cashout: $30 million.
Item. May, 1982: Leon Levy and his partners agree to sell Oppenheimer & Co., the huge mutual fund and brokerage company, to Mercantile House Holdings plc. for $300 million. Levy is still regarded as one of the most astute "special situations" investors of his generation and has enjoyed continuing success as a private investor.
Estimated net worth at cashout: $15 million.
Item. January, 1982: Commodities trader Marc Rich flees the U.S. with the IRS in pursuit. During the so-called oil shortage of the 1970s, Rich created a pe-

troleum trading empire. Now a Spanish citizen, he is negotiating a settlement of U.S. tax claims.

Estimated net worth at cashout: $100 million (tax-deferred, pending extradition).

Item. April, 1985: Congress demands an investigation into corporate takeovers financed with "shaky" junk bonds. Mike Milken—a Los Angeles–based broker for Drexel Burnham Lambert—is the number-one salesman of these high-risk, high-yield securities. His client book? A rogues' gallery of stock market operators on the sell side and aggressive financial institutions on the buy side.

Estimated net worth at cashout: Remains to be seen.

Item. April, 1972: William Simon leaves Salomon Bros., selling out his minor partnership interest for a modest $1.2 million. After a brief stint as Treasury Secretary, Simon embarks upon a third career as a private investor. In 1982, Si-

mon walks away with a $200 million stake from the initial public offering of Gibson Buzza Greeting Cards Inc.

Estimated net worth at cashout: If this guy cashes out again, nobody else will have any money left.

Each of the heroes whose stories you've just read began as young up-and-comers in financial services. Each capitalized on a particular brokerage activity at an opportune moment to accumulate millions. Some have already taken their money and run.

This is what cashing out is all about.

Burning Ambition

Take a close look at your life as a successful broker. You're living well. You drive a nice car—so does your spouse. Your home is beautiful. You've got it all, and everybody knows it.

DONALD T. REGAN: BROKER EXTRAORDINAIRE

New Year's Eve, 1980. Seven thousand Merrill Lynch account executives from around the world crowd into New York's Madison Square Garden. The occasion? One of the great moments in financial services history. A great man is moving on. The man: Donald T. Regan, the architect of the "thundering herd's" rapid growth during the sixties and seventies. In that smoke-filled arena, the roaring crowd fell silent for a moment as Don's production number was officially retired. Those three digits still hang from the rafters, befuddling Knicks and Rangers fans, but an inspiration for those who have a license to sell. Here's a brief recap of Don's rise to the top:

1940—Graduates from Harvard and joins the Marine Corps.
1946—Mustered out of the Corps as a Lieutenant Colonel and joins Merrill Lynch as an account executive trainee.
1952—First move into management, in charge of over-the-counter trading.
1954—Named a general partner.
1964—After managing several branches, he returns to the home office as an administrative officer and executive VP; has Quotron machine removed from his executive office.
1968—Named president.
1971—Named chairman and CEO.
1973—Merrill goes public, Regan named CEO of the new holding company.
1977—Merrill Lynch introduces the first Cash Management Account.
1980—Regan retires and becomes U.S. Treasury Secretary.
1986—Regan becomes White House Chief of Staff.

"Time to establish a beachhead."—Don Regan

Of course you need these outward signs of affluence. Your clients and firm expect them. And you depend on material possessions to bolster your confidence and to drive you to achieve ever higher levels of commission production.

So what's the problem? To find out, take a look at your personal balance sheet. If you're like most hard-charging brokers, it's not a pretty sight. You're probably in hock to your firm and to your bank. You may be making $150,000 a year, but you're spending $200,000. American Express plans to issue you a Kryptonite Card to keep up with your spending.

You have experience,

There's no time for drugs in the intense world of financial services.

product knowledge, and a full book of accounts going for you. But you can't stay ahead and you can't afford to quit.

It's time for you to take a bold, decisive step in the direction of true financial independence. It's time for you to head for cashout.

If you don't make your move soon, you'll end up like many other brokers whose careers plateau after they've been in the business for five to ten years. Look at your colleagues and you'll see what we mean.

There's Larry over in the corner. His baldness cure backfired. He not only bought the product, he put all his clients into the company that makes it. His desperate attempt to pull out of a nosedive failed.

Or take Wanda. She's lost her will to sell. Her production has dropped and she's a regular at the mandatory weekly sales meetings. She sneers at enthusiasm and hasn't added a name to her client book in months. Her income hasn't only

plateaued—it's plummeted.

Then there's Bill. You don't know him, but you read about him in the paper. He's doing time in a minimum-security federal pen. His T-bill arbitrage tax-shelter scheme didn't work.

These brokers got trapped on the treadmill of financial sales. They may not know it, but they are suffering from the dreaded, largely incurable affliction known as broker burnout.

Broker Burnout

Before burnout, most brokers are confident, relaxed, well-spoken and satisfied pillars of the community. When burnout hits, brokers turn into frazzled, insecure sociopaths.

The first sign of burnout is a sharp drop in a broker's production. The broker responds with irrational des-

These brokers, still in their early thirties, provide chilling evidence of the harsh physical toll of broker burnout.

peration: he begins to put in long hours at the office.

This extra time is spent in vain. All of his efforts to drum up business will fail—reinforcing his frustration. Indeed, burnout victims' negative attitude isn't limited to themselves. They find fault with almost everything—their firm, their colleagues and any reasonable investment idea that is proposed in the office.

Next to go is a broker's home life. Happy marriages fall apart as the broker pulls into a psychological shell, losing all interest in sex and restaurants. The children

soon feel the effects—they generally drop out of school and devote their lives to selling Amway products.

Because no made-for-TV movies have yet been made about broker burnout, spouses and kids have no way of knowing what's wrong. That's why many spouses often confuse burnout symptoms with the usual behavior of their broker/partner in a bear market. Who can tell the difference between a super-achiever putting in extra hours and an RR on the road to self-immolation?

In its advanced stages,

burnout saps a broker's most important psychological quality: his sense of self-esteem. To a high-powered salesman, self-esteem is a funny thing. When he's got it—nobody cares. And when he doesn't—nobody cares either. This vacuum means that there's no support mechanism for a burned-out broker, nothing to prevent the broker from drifting slowly away from reality.

Victims reject any marketing focus. As we've seen, some start chasing gigantic deals. Others become production zombies—only barely able to hit mandated minimum-commission quotas.

You might think that brokerage companies would do something to prevent burnout. They don't. Burnout can work to their benefit. Wall Street executives know that the half-life of a brokerage career is less than ten years. They have little incentive to hang on to a rep whose production has peaked.

Firms want their clients to be loyal to the organization—not the broker. In fact some companies would be happy to see the bottom 80 percent of their sales force trade their entrepreneurial independence for a small but steady salary.

A Better Way!

So how did William Simon, Marc Rich, Leon Levy, Mike Milken and Donald Regan avoid burnout and become legends?

How did our heroes overcome the travails of their times—ranging from the demise of fixed-rate commissions to massive FBI manhunts—and go on to become rich and famous?

Each realized that the way to cashout is to personally gain control of one or more of the basic profit functions of a financial

DO YOU HAVE IT?: BROKER BURNOUT TEST

If you're worried about burn-out, answer the following questions and check your responses with the chart below:

☐ Have you recently spent a lot of time cleaning your gun collection?

☐ Have all your subscriptions to important business publications expired?

☐ Do you physically resemble the Elephant Man?

☐ Do you ever feel like taking every dime you own and risking everything on a long-shot options play—just for the hell of it?

☐ Do you no longer care about keeping your client and lead lists alphabetized?

☐ Do you secretly miss double-digit inflation?

☐ Do you regret that every state in which you are registered to sell securities has a set of your fingerprints on file?

☐ Are you on fire?

☐ Is self-esteem something you only read about in your daughter's copy of *Seventeen* magazine?

☐ Do you ever worry that when a client puts you on hold he is really racing over to your office to sneak up behind you and smash your face into a Quotron machine?

☐ Have you noticed that when you play the lottery your production number is never lucky?

☐ Have you begun to notice how stupid people really are?

Scoring

Add up the number of questions to which you answered "yes," and check the total against the following table.

0–3   You're too relaxed. Have you considered going to law school at night?

3–6   You're almost at the ideal stress level. Consider working an extra two hours a day.

6–8   You are under considerable stress. Switch to an all-bran diet and plan for major changes in your life.

8–11 This is the stress danger zone. Have your sales assistant dial 911 for immediate help.

services organization: commissions, fees from money management, trading, deal-making and, yes, information.

Each of our heroes put his energies into one of these profit functions and ended up with an equity position in a financial services organization. Then they sold out those positions at an opportune moment. They bought in low and sold high.

Don Regan—a canny ex-Marine—became the ultimate company man. Management turned out to be Regan's route to big money and enormous power. No broker could ever produce enough commission to match what old Don pulled in on override as an executive in a massive selling pyramid. Don climbed to the top and then made the damn thing bigger.

A similar path to cashout was followed by Leon Levy, although, much to his discredit, he was never a customer's man. Starting in research, he built the reputation and assets of Oppenheimer mutual funds to the point where in 1969 he observed, "People look at us as a fund with a firm tacked on."

Marc Rich and Mike Milken, our youngest heroes, have yet to cash out completely (how do they manage to pay their bills?). But both men have proved that they can make money by gaining control over a valuable commodity. Rich traded petroleum when the world thought that oil was better than money. Milken, underwrites junk bonds at a time when no one can tell the difference between funny money and the real thing.

Bill Simon is the most adept of them all—he's already cashed out twice. As a deal-maker he is cutting against the grain of one of this century's most persistent trends: a shift of corporate ownership from individuals to institutions. Simon is accumulating with partners what may soon be one of the country's largest privately owned industrial organizations. To what end? Why, to sell high and cash out yet again!

So how about you? How do you avoid burnout? And how do you achieve cashout?

Keep in mind that your own cashout strategy should be designed to match your current situation and the prevailing market environment. It's too late to join the Marines and storm beachheads with Don Regan. If you try to corner the oil market like Marc Rich, the only people who will be impressed are Winnebago owners.

Your first step is to determine that you don't want to be a stockbroker for the rest of your life. Because if you spend your financial services life promoting the ideas of others, you're nothing but a capitalist's fool.

If you're on the verge of burning out, it's not because of who or what you are, it's because of *where* you are.

If you're career isn't moving, maybe you should!

Headhunters: Positioning Yourself

Many in the industry still believe that a good way to launch a cashout gambit is to find a job at a new firm, preferably a bigger one. Changing firms may end up being nothing more than horizontal mobility, but it should at the very least give your income a short-term boost.

Making the switch is

Brokers preparing to jump to a new firm (white men always run at the first sighting of a headhunter).

easier than you might think. You won't have to go out and grovel like you did to get your first job. Hardworking flesh peddlers (aka headhunters) will do the work for you.

As soon as you get established in the business, you'll start getting calls from these employment go-betweens. Make good use of the headhunter of your choice—even brokers who have no intention of changing jobs make a point of visiting a headhunter periodically, just as homeowners or coin collectors get their holdings appraised.

Headhunters sell brokers on the greener pastures at the firm next door. The green they flash is a compensation package full of accelerated payouts, up-front bonuses, forgivable loans and gross commission targets. But don't expect any career counseling from headhunters—what they're interested in is the commission they collect for delivering you to a new employer.

Headhunters generally set up meetings with prospects in hotel suites. Forget about the vaguely kinky implications. The location is picked for your own protection. Headhunters are known and employed by every manager in your town, including your own.

Once you're knee-to-knee with a headhunter in a neutral executive suite, spell out what you want. Always bid high and ask for more than you are likely to get. Insist on a six-figure signing bonus or a private office in the firm's San Francisco branch. If you haven't been asked to leave by this point, you are a hot prospect. So demand registered assistants, a large equity stake and paid vacations before hightailing it to the elevator and the nearest fern bar.

Never get overexcited by the wooing of a headhunter. The best you can hope for out of all your trouble is a job.

You've already got one of those.

Former President Gerald R. Ford is named honorary BOM–ROP of the Shearson/American Express Palm Springs office.

Management: Another Get-Rich-Slow Scheme

Cashing out on the management track is a long-term effort that takes you away from the entrepreneurial free-for-all and puts you into the more controlled world of administration.

For a retail rep, the best way to go into management is to become a branch office manager, better known in the trade as a BOM–ROP (branch office manager–registered options principal). Like a modern-day slaveowner, a BOM–ROP owns a piece of the brokers who work for him, because part of his compensation comes in the form of an "override" on the brokers' commissions. The simple arithmetic of the override bonus drives a manager to

GREAT MOMENTS IN FINANCIAL SERVICES HISTORY

May 17, 1792:
Twenty-four brokers agree to form first organized stock market in New York. They meet under a buttonwood tree at what is now 68 Wall Street.

March 10, 1815:
First NYSE stock listings published in a daily newspaper, the *Commercial Advertiser*.

March 16, 1830:
Dullest day in the history of NYSE. Only 31 shares traded: 26 shares of United States Bank, and 5 shares of Morris Canal and Banking Co.

March, 1848:
Eighty-two Illinois businessmen meet to found the Chicago Board of Trade.

November 15, 1867:
Stock tickers first introduced.

October 23, 1868:
NYSE memberships made salable. Previously, brokers had a reserved 'seat' until death.

November 13, 1878:
Telephones introduced on NYSE. Money talks for the first time.

December 15, 1886:
First million-share day (1.1 million shares).

January 23, 1895:
NYSE recommends that listed companies distribute annual reports. Paper stocks rally.

July 31, 1912:
Economist Milton Friedman is born.

July 31, 1914:
NYSE closed through December 11—due to World War I.

October 30, 1924:
Sliding scale of commission rates adopted.

The founding of the NYSE. "A buttonwood tree grew there then, and beneath it they drew up this agreement."

October 29, 1929:
Stock market crash—16,410,000 shares traded. Air bags installed on all NYSE seats.

September 2, 1930:
Faster ticker installed (500 characters per minute).

March 6, 1933:
Bank Holiday. All exchanges closed.

May 27, 1933:
Securities Act of 1933 enacted. Fraudulent sales of securities prohibited. Investors now have the right to demand full financial disclosure. The golden era of securities sales comes to a bitter end.

June 16, 1934:
Glass-Steagall Act enacted—requiring complete separation of investment and commercial banking. So-called "Chinese Wall" erected.

June 6, 1934:

Securities Exchange Act of 1934 enacted, establishing the Securities Exchange Commission and beginning the modern era of securities regulation.

June 4, 1953:

First corporate member of NYSE—Woodcock & Hess Co.

September 14, 1960:

Ministers from five petroleum exporting nations meet to swap Elvis records and form OPEC, a trade association.

Dec. 1, 1964:

New ticker (900 characters per minute).

Dec. 30, 1970:

Paper crunch—the infamous Back Office Crash. Congress passes the Securities Investors Protection Act.

July 27, 1971:

First publicly traded member firm is listed on NYSE—Merrill Lynch.

1893: The first boiler-room operation founded in basement of the Philadelphia Bourse.

1929: Smoking gunslingers? The 1929–30 NYSE rifle team.

April 26, 1973:

The Chicago Board Options Exchange opens for business as the world's first listed options exchange.

Apr. 30, 1975:

Fixed-rate commissions abolished. Now referred to as May Day.

Jan. 19, 1976:

New ticker (36,000 characters per minute).

September 30, 1980:

The Wall Street Journal becomes America's favorite daily newspaper as its circulation surpasses 1.8 million.

Aug. 18, 1982:

First 100-million-share day on NYSE (132.7 million shares).

March 28, 1985:

"Turn the bull loose!" Ronald Reagan becomes the first sitting President of the U.S. to visit the floor of the NYSE.

hire more brokers or to move up to regional management to increase the number of RRs producing for him.

Managers always come from the ranks of producers: they are brokers at heart, not professional managers. Upper management keeps its eyes on reps who increase their business above industry standards. Before these RRs begin to earn too much in commissions they are invited to join management.

Oddly, brokers who produce really big commissions are seldom considered for management positions. They are worth more to their firms as producers. RRs are numbers, not people.

So what are the big boys upstairs looking for when they decide to give a broker his own branch?

1. Three years or more in the business.
2. Gross production of $200,000.
3. Leadership experience, such as coordinating a product program or training new RRs.
4. Management experience in a previous career or no felony convictions within the past six months.
5. Someone who has actually read *In Search of Excellence*. (To show that you are contemporary management material, compose your own company song, write yourself a congratulatory memo and then lay yourself off.)

If you do become a manager, be sure to move on to a new slot before disaster strikes and your reputation is besmirched. Whether it is a headhunter raid on your brokers or back-office embezzlement, a BOM–ROP doesn't want to get hung with the bum rap.

Cashout hero Don Regan didn't dillydally around in his first posting—branch manager of Merrill's branch in Washington, D.C. (But he did stay long enough to join the exclusive Burning Tree Country Club—his first introduction to the inner circle of the capitol's elite.)

So why's it worth considering a move to management? Branch managers at national wire-houses can expect to earn $100,000 or more. But in major branch offices of a high-powered firm you can go after real money, say $1 million in a good year. More importantly, someday BOM–ROP could spell R.I.C.H. –C.E.O.

Starting Your Own Firm

But then again, why not *start* at the top?

If you've always wanted to be your own boss, you should consider moving into the cashout zone by starting your own firm. You could end up with a multimillion dollar payoff. At the very least, you'll have the satisfaction of having your own name on the office door.

Take the case of Marshall Cogan, Roger Berlind, Sanford Weill and Arthur Levitt, Jr., four adventurous young brokers who in the mid-1960s teamed up to start a firm with barely $100,000 in capital. Who recognizes any of their names now or remembers the score of failing firms they accumulated to become Shearson Lehman/American Express. Of course it took these boys twenty years to make it big. Some of the partners fell by the wayside before the big score, but the survivors parlayed their little firm into one of the biggest cashouts in Wall Street history.

Are you tired of splitting your gross commissions with a firm that is no longer creative and is burdened by a deadening bureaucracy? Are you tired of driving 55 miles per hour on the autobahn? Maybe hopping on the entrepreneurial express is something you should

have tried *yesterday*.

What do you need to get started? The NASD requires $5000 in capital reserves for a firm marketing only limited partnerships. A firm engaged in trading marketable securities like stocks and bonds must meet a minimum capital requirement of $25,000. Applications must be approved by the SEC and by regulators in any state you wish to do business in. Finally, to qualify as a principal of a broker/dealer firm you must pass the NASD Series 24 exam.

What else do you need to know? That's easy:

1. Focus on a high-margin product.
2. Advertising is absolutely essential.
3. Forget about strategic planning—hire an MBA to write your business plan.
4. Rotate your tires every three months for maximum performance.

If you want to cash out before the turn of the century, find an office, print up some business cards, lease a Xerox machine and plug in the phones.

Good luck. You can hire a secretary next week!

Flooring It

If an opportunity to speculate with your own capital in a gutsy and fast-paced setting sounds appealing, you should consider seeking your fortune on the floor of an exchange as an independent trader.

An experienced registered rep should have no problem passing muster as an exchange member. You don't even need that much money—if you can't afford to buy a seat you can always rent one. Exchanges all over the country are eager for energetic young capitalists to join them.

A floor trader must master short-term trading (called scalping) and learn about hedging and spreading his positions' profit from small price changes. These trading techniques would be suicidal for the average investor but they are essential for all floor brokers.

After a short period of trial and error, a floor trader can earn at least three times his capital base. With miniscule overhead and marginal transaction costs, a floor trader has a unique ability to build wealth in financial markets.

Right now you can buy a seat on a struggling futures exchange for less than a good month's paycheck. Lease it to someone else until the Reagan disinflation exhausts itself and then go into business.

Piercing the Suburban Intellectual Bunker

If the thought of talking to another client induces painful bodily ailments, you better get moving fast.

A good way to cure the pain and at the same time advance your prospects for a big score is to start an investment newsletter. You'll never have to make a cold call again and you may end up with an immensely profitable publishing and investment-advisory company.

Your first step is to move to a remote Sun Belt leisure community. A Tempe, Arizona, postmark or the equivalent is an absolute must in this image-conscious business.

You can use your old clients and names obtained from your friends in the brokerage business as an initial mailing roster. This could substantially reduce your start-up costs (publishing experts say that it takes about $50,000 to break into the business).

Start sending out the letter for free. But as tax time approaches, bombard your subscribers with an offer of "a $150 tax-deductible investment in the future." Can anyone afford to turn down both a tax deduction and a dynamite newsletter for $150? Don't dream of pricing your letter for anything less, or it's not worth the tax savings you offer.

Even if you only start with 500 subscribers, you'll gross $50,000. Your only overhead is copying and postage, which should suck up no more than 20 percent of revenues. Set up a telephone hot line as a "special service," and you've doubled your gross revenues again.

Once you really get rolling you can hire a college kid to write the newsletter, while you spend your time cruising the Caribbean in search of sandy beaches and tax havens. Any IRS or SEC investigation will simply serve as free PR for you and your letter. Who knows, if the Dow hits 4000, you might even win a Nobel Prize in economics.

Hitting the big time makes you famous and allows you to rake in more dollars by selling books, tapes and computer software.

The only thing you have to lose is your integrity. Most newsletter types are regarded as quacks by the financial services establishment.

The Big Payoff

If you have read this far and not achieved success as a registered representative, go back to chapter 1.

But for the rest of you, well, what's left to learn? You've cashed out. You're wealthy. And you did it your way.

You may not be a West Texas wildcatter, a Hollywood movie mogul or a fast-food kingpin. You may not be in the Forbes 500. But you, a financial services superstar, have more than cash—you have *cachet*. You have only one client left—and it's you.

You are no longer part of the information economy. Anyone who has cashed out has acquired connections,

knowledge and leverage—in other words, power. Your job is no longer to sift through information or to use information to convince other people to give you their money. Instead, your next move is the one piece of information everyone else would like to have. You are making your own future.

Here are a few helpful hints to keep in mind as you enter the post-cashout phase of your life:

1. Fabulous wealth is, in fact, the only known cure for a hangover.

2. If Richard Nixon invites you to join Manhattan's foreign policy and financial elite at one of his Friday night potluck dinners, always bring tuna casserole.

3. When Louis Rukeyser invites you to become a regular on *Wall Street Week*, insist that you appear on the program by remote satellite hook-up. The show is taped in a town called Owings Mills, Maryland, hardly a spot for a hotshot like you.

4. If you want to get out of the country for a while and soak up some rays, why not do it in style? Buy yourself an ambassadorship in a beautiful, tax-advantaged tropical paradise. But don't go coco-loco: no sunblock properly protects the exposed genitalia of nude sunbathers.

5. When it comes time for your final sales call to eternity, do it with dignity. A full-service hospice is available to all former NYSE registered representatives. Expire in a broker-friendly environment where you can go out with your finger on the trigger and your Quotron blazing. Staffed with professional medical executives and caring consultants, the Broker Hospice is fully bonded and a member of SIPC (Sick Investment Professionals Corporation). That's hospitality!

Your years as a cashout hero will be glorious ones. From your privileged posi-

The Reagan Bull Market has put brokers back on their yachts.

tion, you'll be able to laugh at jerks like Bob Vesco who don't know the joy of an honest dollar or at any poor soul who doesn't have at least ten million of them!

One more thing. Plan to have some fun with your money. Find yourself a good stockbroker and have a ball.

BLOWING BUBBLES

Once or maybe twice in your career a time will come when you and everybody else in the business are making easy money. Financiers will be hailed as national heroes. New MBAs will reject less glamorous pursuits and make a beeline to Wall Street.

During these so-called market "bubbles," any financial product can take on a life of its own. Whether it's stocks, bonds, commodities, tax shelters or mutual funds, the product of the moment will sell itself.

How can this be? Don't try to ponder human nature—if there's a bubble out there, just sit by the phone and sell. If people want tulip bulbs—you're a Dutchman. If they crave caviar, go fishing. But praise be to Allah you are a registered representative and can sell them almost anything they want.

That includes the firm you work for. When the stock mar-

John Blunt (center), the originator of the South Sea Bubble, captivates hungry investors at an early eighteenth century investment seminar.

ket is hot, brokerage companies are steaming. Financial service organizations become prime takeover targets. Call up any big insurance company or Japanese trading group and you'll find a willing investor.

You don't have to be a hotshot investment banker to make the deal. If you can sell a hundred shares of Merrill Lynch you've already got the sales tool that can change your life. You can use the very same pitch to sell your entire company to some foolish corporation eager to diversify into financial services.

You will have an exclusive on this trade because during bull markets everybody else on the street—from CEOs to CFPs—will be too busy hauling in the money ever to consider cashing out.

Setting up a corporate ambush—successful or not—will convince the world of what you already know. You are the greatest salesman in history. A ruthless corporate manipulator and a savvy investor. In short, you are a financial genius.

And if the deal works, your seven-digit finder's fee will make you a rich financial genius.

And all you had to do was blow some bubbles.

EPILOGUE: YOU AND YOUR BROKER

"I want the product—not the salesman. Why should I give a stockbroker my business?"

It's a logical question. You can do just fine with a discount broker who will execute your trades for a fraction of what a full-service broker charges. Perhaps that's why discount brokers—known to RRs as "generic investment services"—have already captured about 20 percent of the retail brokerage business.

Can there be any reason for shelling out up to ten times the cost of a simple financial transaction to your full-service broker?

Yes.

Take the example of the nation's most successful investors. They didn't get rich by ignoring the bottom line, but even savvy corporate raiders like T. Boone Pickens think nothing of shelling out tens of millions for good brokerage advice from a highfalutin RR if it leads to a successful takeover gambit.

You too can experience the sheer pleasure of having

an intelligent, ambitious individual willing to do anything to make you happy. All for a handful of securities transactions.

Having a good stockbroker is like having a financial expert on your personal board of directors. His concern is to cater to your ambitions and to cultivate your assets (let your spouse, lawyer and in-laws worry about your liabilities). What's more, a good broker can do far more than make you money. A full-service broker can also get your derelict kids into private schools, find you tickets to the Super Bowl and even refer you to an honest Mercedes repairman.

How do you find the stockbroker who can take care of some of your most important needs, both temporal and spiritual? Should you throw those commissions to an old college buddy or to your third cousin? Can dear old Dad's customer's man keep you entertained and out of hock?

Of course it's worth trying a broker who has done well for people you know and trust. But keep in mind that your financial objectives are not the same as those of your acquaintances. The same broker who's done good by your aunt with conservative retirement investments might not be the broker you want if you're into structuring backspreads in currency options.

Indeed, finding a good broker is a private matter. And sometimes mutual chemistry is more important than having the same opinion about next quarter's GNP. "You should use the same instincts when you're looking for a broker as you do when you size up a member of the opposite sex at a cocktail party," remarks one veteran industry observer. "Fortunately, investors don't have to do much flirting—there are thousands of brokers out there today on the make for good clients."

What do you do if all the

brokers you're referred to don't seem right for you or if you don't know anyone who has a broker? Your first thought might be to call a local brokerage office and say: "Excuse me, I'd like a stockbroker please." Forget it. If you do this, your call will be handled by a "broker of the day," the salesman assigned to answering all unsolicited calls. A broker of the day is too preoccupied with cranks to exhibit any of the finer qualities you are looking for in a stockbroker.

You will be better off if you take a more indirect approach. Begin by looking through *The Wall Street Journal* or any financial publication. Answer a handful of "no obligation" offers from brokerage firms. This will put your name, address and telephone number on a score of brokers' hot prospects lists. Within days salesmen will start contacting you.

One conversation should be enough to screen out undesirables. If you speak to an incompetent salesman,

dump him immediately. If a broker can't do his own simpleminded job properly, who wants him?

Invite the sharpest candidates to your home or office for a personal interview. A broker's sales patina should be least annoying in an environment you can control. There's no need to interrogate the prospective broker, but don't let the broker control the interview. Establish that you're the boss.

The broker you're looking for is:

1. Smart, but not too much smarter than you.
2. Aggressive, but not impolite.
3. Honest, but not so hung up that he interrupts your enjoyment of market manipulation.
4. Compatible, but with talents that complement, rather than duplicate, your own.
5. Sincere, but not slimy.

The RR who proves to be intelligent, honest and

amusing is your best choice.

Your final step before giving your new broker the nod is to conduct a quick background check on the broker's firm. The NASD, SEC and exchanges can help you pinpoint potential capital problems or criminal tendencies. Unfortunately, Cub Scouts sometimes work for bucket shops, and patholog-

BROKER SCREENING TEST

There are many unknowns facing an investor as he enters the financial markets. He cannot hope to succeed without truly understanding those few things that can be understood. There are two. First, the investor must know himself. Second, he must know his broker. And if more than three of the following eight broker analysis criteria apply, find a new one.

☐ Does your RR wait for you to make a suggestion—and then all of a sudden jump on the idea bandwagon—simply amplifying your own interest?

☐ Does your broker make a practice of observing all religious holidays—even though his only acts of reverence are reserved for German-built automobiles?

☐ Does your broker pay for his own subscription to the *Wall Street Journal*—or is he satisfied with sloppy seconds?

☐ If your broker decided to chuck it all and go scuba diving in the Caribbean for a year, would you join him?

☐ Does your broker habitually arrive at the office late—complaining about all-night Trivial Pursuit parties?

☐ Is your broker a Canadian citizen?

☐ Do you think that he supplements his income with bounties from the IRS?

☐ Do you have to threaten your broker's life to avoid being put on hold?

ical maniacs sometimes become honchos at prestigious firms.

Now that you've found an honest broker you want, how can you be sure that he or she wants you? Unfortunately, the reality of the situation is that what a broker most wants is a client with a lot of money. If you're like most people, that isn't you.

The accepted wisdom in the brokerage business is that there are only one million Americans rich enough to be prime clients. Even if you have a liquid net worth of $50,000 and total assets of $250,000, you're still re-garded by brokers as a "modest" investor.

This doesn't mean that a good broker will turn down anybody who isn't a millionaire. After all, financial services companies spend millions on TV commercials during major sporting events to send out their messages amid the ads for beer and pickup trucks. They want Joe Sixpack's investment dollar.

So even though you may not be a broker's dream client, you can still look forward to a pleasant—and potentially profitable—relationship. Your broker may devote more attention to his

richer clients, but that's fine, just so long as he's willing to pass along the false rumors and half-baked inside information he picks up in his dealings with the high and mighty. This is the basic entertainment staple for any investor.

You can expect your customer's man to become a special kind of friend. There are some things only your broker should know. Even if he says he doesn't want to listen.

Why? Because your stockbroker is someone who uniquely understands the fun and excitment your stash of wealth provides you.

There is no joy in talking about your money to your family; it only provokes arguments. Your friends would find you boorish and boastful if you talked to them about money. But your stockbroker knows enough about money to comprehend your exhilaration, and earns enough on his own to really share in the fun of having it.

Your broker exists to keep you—a good client—happy. Only have-nots or lunatics actually believe that a stockbroker's job is to make his poor clients rich.

Operation Nephew

In your search for a competent broker, you may end up opening an account with a customer's man who turns out to be lazy, incompetent or something worse (your long-lost twin perhaps).

Once you've decided that you've found a loser, move immediately to extricate yourself by asking the branch manager to ship you all of the cash and securities held in your account. This may not happen. Brokerage firms' data-processing facilities tend to break down when a transfer is requested.

Don't bother to argue with the manager, your broker or operations people. Revenge will come soon enough: Operation Nephew can now begin.

Recruit your nephew or any mature-sounding youngster under the age of eighteen to open an account with the RR you have chosen to destroy. Contact with the broker should be made exclusively over the phone. Your nephew should open the account using his own name and social security number—but he should disregard any question about his age by quickly changing the subject to arcane options strategies.

Since your nephew probably does not have a checking account, you must use other means to get money into the new brokerage account. This can be done by shipping bearer bonds to the firm. You will avoid both revealing your identity and committing wire fraud with this funding technique. The greedy broker will himself commit the necessary unethical actions to place the bonds in the account.

Now let your nephew have a field day. Let him trade options, futures, new issues or whatever catches his fancy.

As long as he loses money before his eighteenth birthday the rotten RR is sunk. Any losses in the account are the sole responsibilty of the broker. A minor's signature is not legally binding, and therefore he cannot open a securities account. However, it is the broker who bent the law, not the kid. Therefore the broker must pay for ignoring NYSE Rule 415: "Know your customer."

If you're really lucky, you'll be able to come out with more than your original deposit and a routine pound of flesh. Case in point: If you deposit $50,000 with the broker and he then proceeds to run it up to $100,000 by squeezing the Maine potato futures market, you're broker will be french fried. The futures position will eventually plummet, wiping out the whole investment. The broker will then potentially be liable to pay back all the commissions he earned as he was riding the market up, in addition to the total losses in the account.

What a beautiful way to get some offensive RR (registered rat) to say uncle!

APPENDIX

The Back Office: A Crash Course

The carpeted, open office occupied by you and your colleagues is the dining room where the goodies of the financial world get served up to investors. The area known as the "back office" is the kitchen where all the dirty work gets done.

If you've ever waited on tables in a restaurant, you know that a good relationship with the fry cooks and busboys is essential. The same applies to financial services, where you can't expect to make good tips without the support of the people in the back office—the so-called "vertical assembly line" of securities sales.

Start by carefully observing the goings-on in the room known as the "cage." It is called a cage not because it is a small jail, but because of the tight security demanded by the *wire operator*, *cashier*, and their warden, the *operations manager*. These people make up the back office. The small size of their salaries belies the enormous power they wield over the operations of your office.

The wire operator commands a computer teletype terminal that transmits all ingoing and outgoing order information. If a broker chooses to bypass the wire during the day by executing orders over the phone, he remains in limbo until the wire operator receives "hardcopy" confirmations.

Wire operators work at incredible speed and with great dexterity. Brokers don't mess with these single-minded technicians for fear of upsetting their delicate and frayed nervous systems. Brokers know that an alienated wire operator might subconsciously transpose a few numbers on an order ticket and blow the broker out of the business with trading errors.

Cashiers hark back to the long-gone preelectronic

A broker communicating with his office cashier in the "cage."

A major stock split creates a paper crunch in a typical brokerage office.

days of the brokerage business. Their main job is to credit incoming checks and securities to client accounts. Blue-collar criminals will be sad to hear that most branch offices have outlawed cash as a form of payment for securities purchases. There is more money in the office postage machine than in petty cash.

Dramatic relief from the painstaking back-office routine comes twice a day, when two burly, well-armed representatives of an armored-car company stroll into the branch office. They've come to pick up and deliver documents or securities for the clearing office in New York. They always take time to share a cup of coffee with your cashier. Once you've seen that the cashier keeps company with folks who are packing heat, you'll feel a new-found sense of respect for this key office administrator.

All trades settle on strict timetables, and the cashier's records track the cash and securities that are transacted. At settlement, the customer takes possession of the securities involved, and the seller of the security gets credited with cash. Stocks and bonds settle in five business days if executed in a cash account, and on the next day if executed in a margin account. Options settle on the next day and futures settle on the same day.

Naturally, these different settlement conventions confuse most clients. Some think settlements are found only on the West Bank. In fact, many experienced investors profess not to know what a settlement date is when it comes time for them to make good on trades.

Such confusion jeopardizes a broker's paycheck. A broker doesn't earn his commission on a transaction until the trade has been settled. Customers who do not pay for their transactions on time also unfairly exploit your firm—this is why so-called "free riding" is against the law.

To help RRs keep their customers in line, brokerage firms send threatening telegrams to any client unable to cough up cash or securities on time. Sadly, these necessary reminders sometimes break up marriages and destroy families. A sellout telegram is often the first evidence that a spouse is recklessly gambling away the family nest egg.

Belly dancers or singing clowns don't deliver these barbed wires. Western Union employs a battalion of battle-tested ex-Marines to make sure that the wheels of finance capitalism do not grind to a halt because of some tardy speculator.

At smaller brokerage firms, the RR must chase down his scofflaw clients on his own. This often includes paying for the cost of the telegram—usually about $45.

Why are settlement times and dates so important? Because clients who don't pay on time are in effect borrowing money from your firm. And lending money to clients—better known as margining—is a very serious and profitable part of the brokerage business.

As lucrative as money and security lending is to the industry, RRs do not share in the proceeds. This infamous float is closely monitored by a firm's margin department.

An RR should get to know the margin clerk assigned to his office. This casual friendship may help insure that your firm will never sell out your clients behind your back.

New Accounts/ Order Entry

Client account agreements are a necessary evil in an office dedicated to the pursuit of legal tender. The agreements are simple and usually contain a margin approval, allowing your firm to lend any cash or securities in a client's account at the firm's discretion. Separate agreements and risk-disclosure documents exist for options and futures accounts. Strict adherence to procedure may tax your nerves, but these forms protect you from destruction at the hands of a "wise guy" client.

Entering a *buy order* or a *sell order* is more pleasant—this is how you will make money. You enter orders by filling out an *order ticket*. An order ticket crams a lot of information into a small form. How many of what, at what price, when and where all get recorded for posterity and the SEC.

Computers haven't eliminated all arduous tasks from the job. Brokers are required to keep handwritten client account information *and* a handwritten cross-reference by product! It's the law, although most brokers delegate the responsibility to their secretaries.

Producing brokers quickly forget the back-office lessons

they learned in training. Your more experienced colleagues will pester you with specific questions, wasting your time. This proves that all the details you've been absorbing over the past two months are irrelevant to success in the business.

A superhardened branch office allows for uninterrupted financial services in the event of a nuclear holocaust.

Thomas Edison's simple but ingenious stock ticker was the forerunner of the ultrasophisticated quote machine. Today's technology can provide everything from Flintstones *reruns to the latest line on the weekend football games.*

QUOTRON: A BROKER'S BEST FRIEND

Tickertape parades are back in style for American heroes. But the ticker and its tape haven't been used on Wall Street to transmit stock quotes in decades.

The Quotron machine—a desktop computer terminal—is now the state of the art in financial data transmission. It is an amazing electronic window that allows RRs to monitor financial transactions worldwide.

A standard-issue Quotron enables a broker to 'punch up' any price quote on request. Reps usually program their machines to display continuously prices of stocks, futures or options that they have an interest in.

This instant access also allows brokers to monitor arcane market statistics, such as the TRIN (short-term trading index) or take a peek at the bids and asks of a specialist's limit-order book. Daily or intraday price charts may also be displayed on the terminal in graph form.

Dow and Reuters news items need no longer be printed out on the 'broad tape.' A broker can retrieve individual items or continuously monitor either news service at his desk.

Quotron machines everywhere have these standard features. However, leading brokerage firms use these smart terminals to communicate proprietary information instantly, directly and exclusively to their sales forces.

All of a broker's accounts can be called up. Past monthly statements can be retrieved. And, best of all, client Street names are cross-referenced by position. Every morning a broker can ask his Quotron to list ten accounts with the most cash or margin available to spend that day.

A broker then must look for product ideas. His Quotron enables him to examine his firm's entire inventory of bonds, stocks or tax shelters. Futures or stock recommendations are updated daily. Options strategies are a snap. An RR can construct his own at his terminal with the help of a real-time "option program" or choose from a variety of prepackaged ideas.

Innovation in the processing of information is the hallmark of all successful financial services firms. Brokers regularly stumble onto software experiments being conducted by their firms. RRs working late at night and woozy from a combination of too many cold calls and cold beers are often astounded by the activity on their Quotron machine.

Information never sleeps.